LENINGRAD

LENINGRAD

By Michael Davidson, Lyn Hejinian,
Ron Silliman, and Barrett Watten

Mercury House, Incorporated
San Francisco

The icons representing the authors were inspired by textile patterns found in the book *Revolutionary Textile Design.*

Frontispiece: Conference session. Presentation by Leningrad poet Viktor Krivulin. Second row (left to right): Marianne Zoschenko and Moscow poet Ivan Zhdanov. Front row: Ron Silliman, French poet Emmanuel Hocquard, French poet Henri Deluy, Michael Davidson. Against wall: Arkadii Dragomoshchenko, Barrett Watten. Photo copyright © Viktor Nemtinov.

Published in the United States by
Mercury House
San Francisco, California

Printed on acid-free paper
Manufactured in the United States of America

Library of Congress Cataloging-in-Publication Data
Leningrad/by Michael Davidson . . . [et al.].
p. cm.
ISBN 1-56279-005-6 (paper) : $9.95
1. Leningrad (R.S.F.S.R.)—Description. 2. Authors, American—20th century—Journeys—Russian S.F.S.R.—Leningrad. 3. Glasnost. 4. Leningrad (R.S.F.S.R.)—Intellectual life. I. Davidson, Michael, 1944-
DK552.L388 1991
947'.453-dc20

90-23186
CIP

For Arkadii, Zina, and Ostap Dragomoshchenko

DAVIDSON
SILLIMAN
WATTEN
HEJINIAN

The authors of *Leningrad* have sought to ground the literary movement known as "language poetry" in a sense of community and to connect it to progressive politics and new social theory. This concern is reflected in the text, in which their four alternating voices run together, collectively forming these essays. The authors may be distinguished only by the icons used as a visual key to identify them: a formal element of the text as poem.

The icons representing each writer are inspired by textile patterns designed in Leningrad in the 1920s and 1930s. In this period industrial design was considered a creative medium well suited to ideals of a new proletarian society.

The circular design element common to all four icons is based on a pattern called "The Five-Year Plan in Four Years." The titles and images of many of the patterns reflect a preoccupation with a new style of Soviet life and the dynamic rhythm and beauty of industrial processes. This art played an important role in the socialist ideology of Russia in the postrevolution period.

AN INTRODUCTION

Written into my journal on March 13, 1989, at the end of a month-long stay in Leningrad, is a first draft of the translation I had been asked to make of a letter of invitation prepared by officials at the Leningrad branch of the Soviet Cultural Fund. I would bring the letter back to the United States the next day. The first paragraph reads:

> *Dear Michael Davidson, Lyn Hejinian, Ron Silliman, Barrett Watten:*
>
> *The board of the creative laboratory Poetic Function in affiliation with the Leningrad branch of the Soviet Cultural Fund invites you to take part in the First International Summer School—a conference on problems in contemporary culture. The theme of the forthcoming conference is "Language—Consciousness—Society."*
>
> *The proposed dates for the Summer School are August 9 to 15, 1989, and it will take place in Leningrad.*

The letter goes on to say that the sponsors of the conference anticipate a reply confirming our willingness to attend; they also ask us to provide the information necessary for beginning the process of visa application. It is signed by Arkadii Dragomoshchenko, "Head of the Board." Just below, on the same page, without any break, I have written, "Arkadii suggests I write a Russian novel; you will start with the third chapter, he says, after an epigraph which should be attributed to Kant: *Everything happens so often that speaking of it makes no sense.*"

The history of my collaborations with Arkadii begins six years earlier, in 1983, when I made my first trip to the Soviet Union and had my first exhilarating and unnerving experiences of Russia, a world that seems both very familiar and profoundly incomprehensible. But the logic that has brought about a confluence of a very specific literary scene in the United States with a similarly specific literary scene in the Soviet Union began for me almost ten years before that, in my correspondence with Ron Silliman and Barrett Watten. They had preceded me in reading the great Russian futurists and formalists, and they were, along with other poets, in the process of elaborating the premises for a literary life that was then beginning also to involve me. The works of the futurists and the formalists were by no means the sole material underlying our activities; there were other literary influences, French and, especially, American, and all of them were contextualized by the social and political life of the time and by our responses to the war in Vietnam, the civil rights movement, and then to the women's movement. And I myself, for example, had a fantastic rather than a comprehensive relationship with the works of someone like Velimir Khlebnikov, partially because his work had been only randomly translated and published in the 1970s, but more significantly because I had no Russian context for understanding the scale and intentions (and hence the meaning) of his work.

But certain qualities of our literary scene and of our life within that scene were informed by our understanding of that earlier Russian and Soviet scene, through the literary and critical writings of Khlebnikov, Viktor Shklovsky, Yurii Tynianov, Boris Eikhenbaum, Roman Jakobson, and others. Their emphasis on and investigation into the *constructedness* of a literary text suggested many ways in which we could talk about our own and each other's works, and in a profound way the notion of constructedness had social implications in our lives. We imagined and, perhaps, partially succeeded in building an intellectual and literary scene outside the traditional sanctioning institutions (principally universities). A desire for aesthetic discovery and aspirations for its social potential—for the relevance of poetry and the kinds of thinking that poetry requires—resulted in the founding of several literary presses, the creation of a radio show, the development of talk and discussion series, the writing of essays, criticism, prose, and poetry, and a social life that flourished (and still does) around these activities, involving many of us who came to be known as the *language poets.*

In May 1983, when I left for the first trip to the Soviet Union, the third issue of *Poetics Journal*, on "Poetry and Philosophy," edited by Barrett Watten and myself, had just come out. Originally, the trip seemed coincidental to our literary life in the United States, and maybe it would have been if conditions in the Soviet Union had been different. But because of the particularly oppressive political atmosphere felt by artists of all kinds during the early 1980s in the Soviet Union, an intense and intimate intellectual "underground" existed. And because I was traveling with my husband, Larry Ochs, and the other members of Rova Saxophone Quartet, an avant-garde group that had been invited to Leningrad and Moscow by "fans," musicians and critics who were "unofficial" and in several cases officially "banned," we found ourselves visiting members of this underground. We arrived in Moscow and were met by Alexander Kan (an influential music critic and the founder of the unofficial Leningrad Contemporary Music Society), Sergei Khrenov (the editor of a *samizdat* magazine of translations that was presenting the first taste of writers like Roland Barthes, Jacques Derrida, Robert Creeley, and Julia Kristeva), Boris Grebenshchikov (then as now a cult hero and the most famous of the poet-singers in the rock scene, although at the time he wasn't allowed to play in public), Sergei Kuryokhin (the great pianist and genius behind the musical theatricality of the group Popular Mechanix), and Alexander Lipnitsky (then playing underground only, now a member of Zvuki Mu). We would spend three days in Moscow, Rova would play two concerts, and then—we were told—we would go by overnight train to Leningrad, where Arkadii Dragomoshchenko and the poets and musicians of Leningrad awaited us.

The situation in Leningrad was complicated by several factors. Rova's concerts in Moscow attracted very large crowds, and the city officials in Leningrad were wary, not just of the size of the audience but more probably of its potential for bringing together artists and intellectuals who had much in common with each other. When we reached Leningrad, we learned that the officials had canceled the Leningrad concert.

I met Arkadii Dragomoshchenko the next day on the Dvortsovaya Embankment near the Winter Palace and accompanied him to his flat in the northern part of Leningrad, where, with gestures, a Russian-English/English-Russian dictionary, and the help of a friend who spoke some English and of British writer Michael Molnar, who is fluent in Russian, we had a first conversation—and I think we had some intuition about what this meeting meant.

I had brought some copies of my own books and of books by Ron, Barrett, Michael, and others, as well as copies of *This* magazine, which Barrett edited. I gave these to Arkadii. In the months that followed, Sergei Khrenov, Vladimir Kucheriavkin, and Mikhail Khazin would begin to translate works from the magazine.

Arkadii Dragomoshchenko was one of the founders of a peculiar organization called

Club-81 (named for the year 1981 in which it began)—peculiar in being an organization of writers not "officially" recognized as such but allowed "officially" to meet. In their meetings they could present readings, discuss works, and "negotiate for the possibility of publication," although they could not publish or be published. Their meetings took place at the Dostoyevsky House, where the novelist had lived and which, being a state museum, was under the control of the KGB. During that first evening at Arkadii's flat, we were told to remain silent while Arkadii telephoned to the KGB person in charge and arranged for a concert by Rova to take place following a poetry reading the next evening. The unofficialness of the occasion, the appropriate conjunction of poetry and music, and the ironies inherent in the conditions under which it occurred, were auspicious. This was also my first experience of the layered logics that guide events and condition situations there—my first experience of the disruptive, compelling, "surreal reality" that Ron, Barrett, Michael, and I encountered in 1989.

During the years that followed my first visit, Arkadii and I collaborated on a number of projects, including a film script, a theater piece, poems, and translation and publication of each other's work.

The same notion of a poetry of consciousness—a poetry, for example, with intentional poetics—that is essential to the language poets and that for us is supported by models from the Russian futurists and formalists, is at the center of the circle called

Poetic Function in Leningrad. The group also includes Moscow poets whose aesthetics are related to Arkadii's—Aleksei Parshchikov, Ilya Kutik, Nadezhda Kondakova, Ivan Zhdanov, Vladimir Aristov, Olga Sedakova, and others. Poetic Function came into existence in 1989 with the intention of opening discussions about aesthetics and consciousness—now that it was possible, in the era of *glasnost,* to do so. During the month I spent in Leningrad, the first issue of the journal *Poetic Function* was being edited, and the idea of an international symposium was discussed. It was to include linguists, philologists, semioticians, and poets. Arkadii knew Ron Silliman, Barrett Watten, and Michael Davidson from a visit he had made to the United States in 1988, and he and other members of Poetic Function had translated some of their critical writing and selections of their poetry. The theme, "Language—Consciousness—Society," was intrinsic to their work, to mine, and to that of some of the writers and scholars from Soviet Georgia, Uzbekistan, France, Latvia, China, Armenia, and Russia who were initially invited. The Cultural Fund in Leningrad, under the directorship of First Secretary R. S. Milonov, agreed to sponsor the event, and the Fund's Aleksei Adashevsky became the coordinator, with Arkadii acting as the aesthetic director.

With travel grants from the University of California and from the Fund for U.S. Artists at International Festivals and Exhibitions, Michael Davidson, Ron Silliman, Barrett Watten, and I were able to attend the symposium. This collaboration is about that week, about juxtaposition, happenstance, double vision, vistas, and a flow of observations and expectations kept in suspense. I've been back since, but I don't know any more.

The trip itself took place during that brief window in world history between the Tiananmen Square massacre in Beijing and the fall of the Berlin Wall and the Eastern bloc. Anthropologist Vladimir Malyavin, whom I first met when he offered to buy me a lunch of boiled beef and sliced cucumber in the minuscule basement café of the Composers Union, had himself been in Beijing at the time of the rebellion. He had been studying the persistence of Christianity in Chinese rural communes. This curious juxtaposition of details was typical of our experience: an absence of consumer goods and the nature of soft currency have conditioned many Russians toward a spontaneous generosity—there is no point in hoarding money—that seems even more pronounced in the face of so much scarcity. The collapse of communism pervaded nearly every conversation, tinted always by a deep Russian pessimism, and the passionate interest of Soviet intellectuals in religion and in various forms of mysticism repeatedly confronted us.

Before we even arrived, events (in the form of United Airlines) had conspired to remind us of just how far behind we were leaving the familiar world. United had canceled our short flight from San Francisco to Los Angeles, so that Michael and I—unable to find either Barrett or Lyn, who had our visas—scrambled to board another carrier to LAX. There, in that huge terminal whose omnipresent multilingual public address system undoubtedly inspired *Bladerunner*'s vision of a media-saturated future, we found our comrades and made our way to Helsinki. Barrett and Lyn's luggage, however, headed for Seattle. This we discovered thirteen hours and ten time zones later.

The next day, having made our way through the dour airport and customs line at Leningrad's remarkably small international terminal, Aleksei Adashevsky waved us into a trio of chauffeured black Volgas (on loan, we presumed, from the KGB), and we sped down country roads toward the city. The impact of a demand economy was immediately visible—there were no suburbs, since suburbs imply the presence of unplanned development. One moment you were in the country and the next amid the late-modernist block apartments that make up the outer rim of Leningrad. On the boulevard people queue up in lines outside of stores whose windows lack advertising and so appear more like storefront medical clinics in the United States. In smaller numbers, people queue up also in front of refrigerator-sized water dispensers, each of which has one or two glasses being used over and over again, or crowd around issues of *Pravda* wheat-pasted onto walls. The Volga that Michael and I share barrels through the streets, at one point riding up onto a traffic island (if that is really what it is) to bypass a stalled military truck, pedestrians scattering out of our path. As we move toward the older inner city (in this detail more than any other Leningrad mimics a European metropolis), we begin to glimpse for the first time the oversized Italianate palaces that form the husk of the city's tsarist heritage, noting their curiously garish pastel colors—lemon yellow, cranberry red.

Like Arkadii Dragomoshchenko, I was a "victory baby" of the Second World War, born in 1946. His father, a career army officer, served in the Soviet Union's European client states after the war. Mine, a radio operator in the navy, became first a police officer—in the USSR he would have stayed in the military—and, when it was no longer possible for him to hold down a job in that profession, a drifting laborer who would die from burns after a factory explosion at the age of thirty-eight. Less than three weeks before his death, I had greeted the dawn of my eighteenth birthday in a Greenwich Village café by reading a *New York Times* account of an incident said to have occurred the previous day in Indochina's Tonkin Gulf.

The impact of the Vietnam War on one generation of American intellectuals cannot, and should not, be discounted. It dramatically accelerated the growth of the American left beyond the civil rights movement. By 1970, however, I was, like many other student activists, weary of anti-intellectualism posing as spontaneity and wary of the groundless and narcissistic revolutionary hubris that characterized too much of the new left. It was at that moment that much of the left in America, for the first time in a generation, began to study versions of Marxism seriously, beginning with Marx and Lenin but also including Antonio Gramsci and the Frankfurt School.

The result in the United States was a new democratic Marxism that proved open first to structuralism and later to poststructuralism. As poets openly committed to the idea of poetry as an intellectual practice,[1] Lyn, Michael, Barrett, and I were variously engaged with these discourses, each of us quite differently and all with degrees of skepticism. Thus, I had read Roland Barthes's *Writing Degree Zero,* a reply to Sartre's *What is Literature?,* not as an apolitical apology for an imagined autonomy of letters, but as a response that actually historicized both writing and the social uses of language. This was a framework that led me back through Roman Jakobson, whom Claude Levi-Strauss had discovered teaching at the New School for Social Research when both were in exile during the Second World War, to Jakobson's own earlier teachers, both scholars (such as Shklovsky and Tynianov) and poets (including Khlebnikov and

[1] Rather than as the versification of persona, for example, which has been the United States's equivalent of an "official poetry" for the past thirty years.

Mayakovsky). When, in 1982, the first issue of *Poetics Journal* published Richard Sheldon's translation of Shklovsky's "Plotless Literature,"[2] I read it much as I read *Writing Degree Zero* twelve years before: as though the text were speaking of my own poetry directly.

This, however, is not the Marxism of which Leningrad poets speak, nor with which Russians have had to contend for more than seventy years. It is not only that a young poet, such as Ilya Kutik, may think of Shklovsky as just a compromising survivor who ended his days as the grand old screenwriter of Soviet television, nor is it any simplified idealization of capitalism confused as democracy—in fact, we found very little of that—or even the curious inversion of energy that pervades Russian society, where people sullenly devote the minimum amounts of labor necessary to any job, in turn for which long hours in lines become obligatory to obtain even the most simple goods. The woman who set up a card table in the plaza outside of the Winter Palace from which to sell individual tampons is for me a figure of scarcity before she is one of entrepreneurship, an index of the complexity of the transition in which Soviet society was already enveloped in August 1989. No less complex was the communal flat occupied

[2] Pp. 3–24. Benjamin Sher's translation is now readily available in Shklovsky's *Theory of Prose* (Elmwood Park, Ill.: Dalkey Archive, 1990), 189–205.

by theater critic Olga Khrustalyeva on Ulitsa Dzerzhinskovo in a building that, ten years earlier, had been used to "house" prisoners of the KGB, one of whose other occupants (either a grandmother or a great-aunt), a one-time dancer with the Kirov Ballet, had seen a revolution, two world wars, and now this curious and dangerous implosion of a society, all within the confines of this city.

For decades, Soviet authors have had to live through the schizophrenic distinction of official and unofficial writing, one group receiving incomes and publication with tens of thousands of copies while the latter's work existed only in a few typescripts to be passed around among friends. Works in translation have been equally difficult to get into print. One result is that works that have had broad international influence in the West since World War II have appeared only fragmentarily in the Soviet Union. For example, the first collection of Barthes's essays had only recently been published when we were in Leningrad, while Viktor Mazin's *samizdat* version of Derrida's *Of Grammatology* was adapted from Gayatri Spivak's English translation.

Perhaps Derrida would find the indirectness of his book's Russian history ironic. But if so, we did not find out, for of all the French writers originally invited to the Summer School, only two, poets Emmanuel Hocquard and Henri DeLuy, succeeded in wading through the Soviet bureaucracy and reaching the conference. One participant, radical analyst Felix Guattari, was refused admission to the USSR outright. The one overt collective political act of the conference itself, beyond its own sheer existence, was a letter protesting Guattari's exclusion.

Still another impact of the heritage of censorship is that all Russian authors, from Shklovsky to Kutik, have had to develop their own strategies of survival and distribution. In 1989, new possibilities of independent publication were just beginning to open up. An "official" magazine, edited by (and normally publishing only) members of the Writers Union, might now have an "unofficial" issue, identical in format but not catalogued by volume and issue number and now containing both official and unofficial writers. As an American who virtually grew up in the context of a small-press scene that has long been the heart of poetry in the United States, I was surprised at the suspicion with which many Russian poets looked at these new possibilities. Even as they were beginning to make use of the new forms for all they were worth, there was a lingering sense that an independent press was somehow not quite real. Also, as Kutik would later say during a trip to San Francisco, "Five years ago, we only had to read and write and pass around manuscripts. Now everybody is running a reading series, editing a magazine, starting up an independent publishing house, inventing conferences. There's no more time to write!" Today, one year after the conference, Aleksei Parshchikov, who in Moscow had reported for a journal, *Rural Youth*, with a circulation of three million, has a graduate fellowship at Stanford University and Kutik works for the BBC in London.

Just as the Vietnam War transformed American intellectual history and much else, Leningrad is a city that has in many ways been defined by conflict. The centralized rule of the tsars meant that much of the Russian Revolution took place on its streets. The 650,000 who died there during the three-year German siege of the Second World War would fill the city of San Francisco. That number is equal to all of the dead in the American Civil War and twelve times the total of American fatalities in Indochina. Old men—any male sixty-two years old has already reached his life expectancy—wear banks of still-colorful medals that stand out on their dull jackets. The large government building next to the Hotel Leningrad is a hospital whose current inhabitants have only recently returned from Afghanistan. That war itself was something few of the Russians we met wanted to discuss. Somewhat like Stalin, it was a subject to be dismissed the moment it was raised. The sole exception was a linguist who argued that the next world war would pit "the northern countries" against Islamic fundamentalism. In his view, Afghanistan was simply the first incursion. In a society where a vast portion of the army comes from regions with an Islamic heritage, that is a profoundly pessimistic view.

A more common expression of such pessimism was the view that the only outcome of the Gorbachev "disaster"—as *perestroika* is routinely called—must be military in nature. People who did not want to speak of Stalin or Afghanistan were perfectly willing to speculate about a coup, so that much of what we saw in the way of the development of new institutions, such as independent journals or the first exhibition of women's art in Leningrad since the 1920s, began to appear as attempts to define terrain that, in the event of a change in government, might prove defensible. This lent everything an enormous sense of urgency.

An even more ominous heritage of Leningrad's history of conflict is racism. On the second day of the conference, several of us rushed through a late-afternoon downpour to a nearby restaurant. Inside, as we waited for our food, a group of young drunks approached our table and proceeded to threaten us in broken English because Parshchikov "looked" Jewish. We had already learned at the Architects Union the night before that Russian eateries don't have a custom of eighty-sixing out-of-control alcoholics. Had Zina Dragomoshchenko not intervened when she did, the narrative would have turned ugly. Nor was this the only instance we saw of racism—even at the conference some Russians snickered at the "cracker" accent of an Armenian scholar.

The other major heritage of Leningrad's history of conflict that is visible to outsiders is infrastructural. One of the most common words in print in Leningrad is *remont,* meaning repairs; this word is placed over any number of buildings, facilities, and roads that are closed. Outside of town, Catherine's Palace, which the German army first occupied and then devastated in retreat, has still been only partially rebuilt. In 1989, the main department store on Nevsky Prospekt was *remont.* So was the Lenin Museum. The street where we were holding our conference was torn up, with hardly any sign of work being done. Next door to the Composers Union, a pink apartment building where Vladimir Nabokov had been born was gutted and under repair, although the only work done while we were there occurred during Barrett's reading—at nine in the evening on a Saturday. A block away, the Hotel Astoria and the town hall were both undergoing reconstruction. One year later, the poet Kit Robinson, himself just back from Leningrad, shows me his photographs. The same boards still cover the entrance to the town hall.

It becomes clear that one of our preoccupations in this book is the social space of a great city. On the one hand, that space is completely familiar, having been given to us over the years through any number of representations—from picture postcards of the Winter Palace in its baroque splendor to scenes from Eisenstein's movies. Moreover, the city is given to us as part of the collective unconscious of a generation growing up during the Cold War. By the time we step off the plane, we have, to some extent, already arrived. And that arrival is itself a product of a new imagination of what the city is, since the changes brought about by *perestroika* include relaxations of restrictions on travel. Even now, over a year later, I return to the city in dreams as a place where I am lost and can neither read the signs nor ask for directions.

As Kristin Ross observes in her book on Rimbaud and the Paris Commune, the subject of social space, like that of poetry, has been much neglected within Marxism. The reasons for this are being debated by a number of scholars now (Edward Soja, David Harvey, Perry Anderson, Marshall Berman, Kristin Ross, Alice Kaplan, Fredric Jameson), but it is worth pointing out that there are relations between space and poetry that make the two easy to dismiss within the context of historical materialism. Social space implies the stoppage of action, the flattening of history into buildings, squares, parks, and demographics, the reification of labor into factories; poetry implies the sedimentation of discourse in figures of speech and prosodic repetition. Social space is the forum of "unreflective" existence, the movement of masses in the great theaters of commerce and consumption; poetry is the forum of the isolated ego, alienated from its source of sensual pleasure and communality. One is denied importance because it describes the space and not the causes of historical change; the other is made marginal because it turns history into a spatial trope.

But it is within social space and poetry that interventions into instrumental, rationalized life may take place, whether in the form of strikes and street demonstrations or in syntactic displacement and collaboration. It was just such interventions that the Russian formalists studied, although their separation of a discrete notion of "literariness" contributed, to some extent, to the very marginalizations within the left that I have just described. As readers of the Russian formalists as well as of modern history, we came to the city of *Opoyaz* to understand its "formal" contours as lived, rather than represented, experience.

The physical size of Leningrad is, as we all point out, quite overwhelming. Vast areas of public space are given over to squares, grand boulevards, and monuments. At the same time, one discovers an unexpected formal clarity to the city, partly the result of its extraordinary eighteenth-century architecture and formal plan, partly the result of its intimate relation to water—rivers, canals, and tributaries endlessly reflect and diffuse light—and partly the result of color that is applied to buildings with great variation and vividness. But one is overwhelmed, as well, by the people, who are, compared to citizens in most Western cities, visible in masses, whether standing in the ubiquitous lines or walking along the wide boulevards. They are not isolated in cars, as we so often are, and when one gets on a bus or subway, as Lyn observes, they seem to swell up and fill the available space. Physical contact is a pervasive cultural fact. And among them, conversation is more than a vehicle of information; it is a way of life. The intensity of debate, discussion, and argument is visible in all aspects of Soviet life—not the least at our conference, where issues of communication, community, and consciousness are the order of the day. The most conspicuous sign of apprehension on the part of our Russian hosts over the current changes in the Soviet Union is not so much fear of economic change brought about by reform but fear of a loss of that social intercourse in the pursuit of Western economic goals.

This intercourse is also a function of social space, from Arkadii's joke about the destroyed nature of the street in front of the Composers Union to the debate within the conference over the "object status" of language. What is at stake in the linkage of space and discourse is that imaginary topography of Russia that Americans inhabited for so long—a rhetoric of otherness that appeared in physical monuments like the Berlin Wall or Checkpoint Charlie or in the various cartographic representations of a militarized East and West, complete with missile targets, bombing ranges, "satellite" countries, and SAC bases. That is, the environment in which history happens is a discursive as well as a physical space, and every attempt to contain one is an implicit summoning of the other.

All of this has implications for the ways in which "our" poetry relates to "theirs." For our entire early life, as a generation, the Soviet experience has been a stage-managed tragedy served to us through ideological props of unbelievable crudity. Unmasking that crudity (while retaining the truths of Stalinist repression) makes use of the very defamiliarizing techniques with which modern Russian literary theory begins. But while formalism begins by carving out a separate "space" for the device, it has no comparable description of the ideology of that space in history: the fact that literary change happens against the backdrop of epochal events, that genres are born out of the needs of new subjects, that the device often occludes unspeakable acts and needs. Thus, the formalist generation's aesthetic motivation becomes our generation's critical goal, and it is this dimension—art's ability to intervene *in*, not simply *on*, the rhetoric of power—that we retain from the Russian tradition. At the same time, in the stuffy, smoke-filled basement of the Composers Union, outside of the official conference, this utopian goal undergoes crucial modifications as we sit down and begin to talk with the real actors of our own period. It is here, in the unofficial convention sponsored by the unofficial writers, that our collaboration truly begins.

It is hard to give up the universality of one's account of oneself as having been formed by the circumstances of birth in a particular time and place, the American 1950s and 1960s, the period of the Cold War and the Vietnam War. "I"—and this is not autobiography but an introduction to a text as a particular enactment of the poetics of social form—remember the unearthly Oxford English of the announcer on Radio Peking broadcasting its antagonistic messages and picked up on car radio from the other side of the Formosa Straits, messages later to be broadcast from satellites circling the globe designed for that purpose. What was one to think this voice represented of its intentions from "the other side" of the line, the wall, the gap between incommensurate states? Itself seamless, allowing for no interpretative space by which its context might be construed—was this a superior and commanding voice of necessity that could only imply the complete and utter denial of oneself? A voice that one could identify with only in the austere resources of inner being that could survive its challenge? Or a voice that covered over and effaced, rendering unreal and thus highly attractive, a world that could never be known? Such was the power of Cold War antagonism in making subjects doubtful of the compass of their existence that later, when the opening of China to the West took place, we would be forced to recode this uncertainty in different language and would come to know that other world in terms of "Radio Beijing" not from the other side of the "Taiwan Straits." (This experience of linguistic alterity will have surfaced, a decade or two later, as one of the main sources for the focus on, and skepticism about, language in the poetics of the language school.)

There is a substantial literature—often written along romantic, nineteenth-century travel narrative lines—of the reencounter of China by the West in the 1970s. It strikes me that there is not being produced a similar literature out of the reencounter of the

Soviet Union by the West in the 1980s, even if both the complexities of and the desire for that encounter are as real as they were for China. Accounts of the "opening" of the Soviet Union—and our collaboration here is certainly a first moment in this as-yet-undetermined genre—will necessitate other and more difficult figures for interpretation than those of a Third World-oriented neocolonialist fantasy. While it has often been said that since the purported "fall of communism" the Soviet Union has become in reality a collection of Third World countries with nuclear weapons and a subway system, this is an untruth. It is the "Second World"—and what is that? Determining in an accurate way what constitutes this Second World is going to be a major interpretative and theoretical task for the next decade. It is going to have, as well, implications for the West's understanding of itself—particularly with the coincident crisis of the Western Marxism that has developed since the 1960s as a vehicle of its own self-scrutiny.

Of course, an illusion of any encounter with the other world is that there is a universal "person," like Robinson Crusoe perhaps, to present the account of its unknown. For reasons having to do with the figure of the "person" in American poetry, the four poets writing here have in large part dispensed with any notion of the universality or separateness of the place from which such an "I" speaks; this will have implications for understanding a world that cannot be reduced so simply to an opposite for "myself." One way to account for this multiplicity of the person has already been suggested in the recourse to language itself as a way of conceptualizing the world on the other side of the Us/Them divide—one can only identify with language when the world it refers to is unknown. But the question of how one has developed as multiple (in spite of oneself) by virtue of the unattainability of an entire half of the known world is not so simply a matter of language. There is a history of cultural figures that have developed from the Cold War for the dilemma of Us/Them, and these figures have left residual traces that must be renegotiated when faced with the real Soviet Union. To do so is to confront the fantasy and dread occasioned by such denial with real knowledge.

It would be beyond what a writer could say about his or her own work to make a thorough inventory of such traces. But exteriorized onto a thumbnail sketch of recent history certain possible themes develop; doubtless numerous others will be revealed in the process initiated here. "I" remember the Coexistence Bagel Shop in San Francisco from about the time of Khrushchev's "We will bury you" speech at the United Nations. There is indeed a difference in interpretation between what Khrushchev's confidence in the Soviet state meant to him and what it could have meant to me. Suburban bomb shelters were springing up about the time of the Cuban missile crisis, and "I" remember, after having been in one of them, trying to imagine what instantaneous incineration—simply vanishing—would be like (from that moment there was almost a desire in place to find out). The totalization that that historical moment occasioned—a totalization of only the half of the world that one identified with the limits of oneself—would be riveted in place with the assassination of Kennedy the year later, as we know. The benign figure of the Coexistence Bagel Shop would thus have been a small and particular exception to the general fear, but it was one that, in our totalized part-of-the-world, immediately had to be countered and replaced. So Herb Caen's invention of the figure of "beatnik" for the now-marginal patrons of that coexistence would render a desire for exception to our collective fate equal to being an agent for the other side. With this other side as our antagonist, the Cold War desire for a way out could only mean, in identifying with the unknown and forbidden, a denial of oneself.

If I insist on this complexity of self-understanding as the basic figure for our collective account of the Soviet Union, it is because, first, it so clearly accounts for the formal decisions made in writing our text. This book is not in any sense a single-voiced narrative of what a version of "I" saw and did on our trip. The text was written, in a nonlinear sequence, by all four writers; although each section is the work of a single author,[3] each is meant to resonate with and complement the others. It should be somewhat unclear in reading this text just who is speaking, and this strategy seems not simply to reinforce the dilemma of the subject I have already discussed but also to comment on other, more (so to speak) authoritative ways of voicing the difference between our world and that of the Soviet Union—a second motive for our stylistic preferences.

Two of these "more authoritative" ways have historical grounds in the necessity of liberal thought to account for the Soviet Union in terms other than the Soviet Union's own (and it must be said that, in any case, the Soviet Union's self-description had been compromised beyond belief since Stalin). The first, positive attempt is that strategy of approximation and apology that seeks a different interpretative horizon for the Soviet state—to be imagined in some way as an extension of the reasonable social functioning the liberal feels himself or herself to embody. An optimistic example of this way of thinking would be the poet Larry Eigner's observation that in either of the two systems there are equal numbers of those whose interests are better served in one system than in the other—societies having a reason, beyond system, that tends to the good. The

[3] The individual writers of each section can be determined by the key that appears on pages vi and vii. It is in the spirit of this collaborative form as much as in the discovery of our other world that an early title for this work was taken from a painting by Ostap Dragomoshchenko, *This Time We Are Both.*

problem for such an explanation would be how to map one's notion of this social rationality—which might as well be one's acceptance of it—onto a rationality one cannot, by definition, know.

A second, negative explanation is given by that view of "totalitarianism" that might be summarized, as it has come down to us now, as "It's all lies." The self-justification of the Soviet state would in this view be—from its origins even before Stalin in Lenin and Trotsky's notion of the party as representative of the social totality, and thus their authorization of Kronstadt and the Cheka—a deformed representation held in place solely by state power. There are too many problems with this view to account for here, but significantly it seems to be a major component of current estimates of the Soviet state by many of the writers and intellectuals we met there—their acceptance of it amounting to a virtual, and to me often uncritical, rejection of all that had gone before. Two problems with it to my mind are these: it makes into epiphenomenon the development of the modern state that even Stalinism certainly represented, and it does not account for the context of belief—not simply repression—that authorized its continuance. (The degree to which this belief is the direct result of repression is simply beyond my capacity to say, although it does not seem possible to imagine the defenses of Leningrad or Stalingrad in World War II without it.)

While the liberal press has been cranking out one or another of these two versions of the Soviet state for the last forty years, poets and other artists have quietly been investigating, by means of identification with the modern art and literature of the Soviet 1920s, ways to avoid either of these (by necessity incomplete) totalizations. Viktor Shklovsky's notions of the "orchestration of the verbal material," "defamiliarization," and the "semantic shift" have seemed to us thus not simply a question of art but one of ethics: the meaning of creative action in a context of some kind (literature, society) that cannot entirely be accounted for. An ethics of partial knowledge is thus available if one cares to read it in that tradition of Russian literature inaugurated by Shklovsky (and this literature now must be seen as much larger than the one that purportedly ended with his recantation of formalism in 1931). The Russian poet Ilya Kutik, a student of Shklovsky's at the Literary Institute in Moscow in the 1970s, agreed with me, in a conversation otherwise notable for its spectacular disagreements, that Shklovsky may well have been both the guiding light behind the notion of the "positive hero" of socialist realism and one of the most implicit critics of its ultimate monstrosity. For me this simultaneity opens up a way of thinking about the partiality of such seemingly totalitarian representations, while for Kutik it was clearly grounds for rejection of Shklovsky and the modernism he theorized. Russian modernism in any case seems, when one considers its mode of organization, very like a key to the Russian state, but the self-conscious partialness of its representations in art—such as Malevich's autonomous squares—is radically at odds with, say, the ubiquitous and clearly unadmired statues of the positive hero Mayakovsky, even if Mayakovsky's recasting as a proto-realist was a direct consequence of his earlier constructivist motives.

It is with this identification, of the partialness of Russian modernism's representation of itself with our admitted partialness of self-knowledge, that the possibility of our correspondence with Russian avant-garde counterparts begins. It certainly does not end there, because while the necessary real of the Soviet Union on the other side of our Us/Them dilemma may be there to reassure us that we can find a self-conscious modernism still in place in some form, the writers and intellectuals we found there seem to have rejected the skeptical claims of *this* modernism entirely, largely because it is perceived by them, in the end, to have served the state. In the place of this modernism has been substituted the radically subjective figure of Osip Mandelstam, believable because he intended no analogy to the state and, exactly, because he died for it. After Mandelstam, interiority seems to be the dominant project of contemporary Russian poetry—an interiority that takes alternating wildly metaphysical and theatrical stances and that would take more than our week of talking to Russian poets to understand. What this interiority means for the conditions of belief that have developed within the context of the Soviet state—and in consideration of its historical disjuncture from its course—can only be speculated on; how could it be directly known? What we have tried to say in the provisional account that follows should be taken in that light. The spaces that can be read between the lines will be the grounds for recurring questions.

I had lost my luggage, and in that sense was about as exposed in my negotiation of the upcoming boundary as I could possibly want to be. On the way to the Helsinki airport for Leningrad, Ron observed that we were now a long way from our beatnik days when we had first met on Telegraph Avenue in Berkeley in 1964. "Let's go to Russia," he said, and we did. This had always seemed an attractive possibility, and now twenty-five years later we had found the means to go. What was on the other side of that line was a palpable reality self-evident and uninvolved in any complex denial of oneself. Still it was a place that the difficult language of poetry, as I was to find out, seemed to have held in reserve as a promise all along.

1

"I can't do this," Barley thought. "I'm not equal to these dimensions."

—John Le Carré,
The Russia House

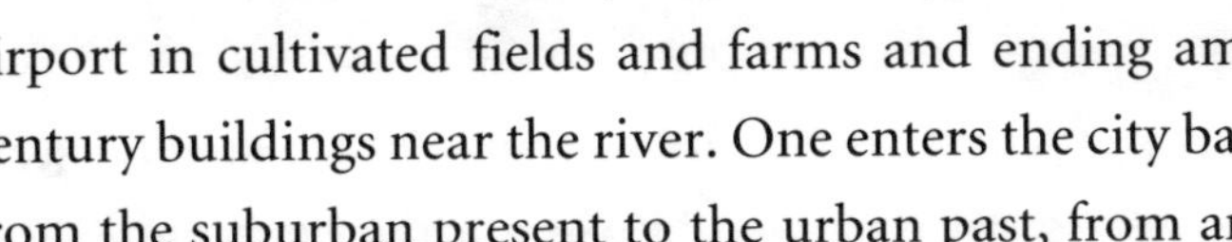

The boulevard slices directly into the center of the city, beginning at the airport in cultivated fields and farms and ending amidst eighteenth-century buildings near the river. One enters the city backwards in time, from the suburban present to the urban past, from anonymous modern apartments to brightly colored, rococo palaces. At the edge of the city the boulevard enters a vast roundabout, in the center of which is a monument to the siege of Leningrad. Giant statues of soldiers and citizens stare at the countryside where the Germans, unable to penetrate the city, bivouacked for three years. Across the street from the monument is an enormous state building of the Stalin era. Its mass is not so much that of height or width as of repetition—a facade of insignias. The same massiveness (but with far greater variation in surface) may be seen in Dvortsovaya Square, ringed on one side by the Winter Palace and on the other by the General Staff headquarters and punctuated in the center by the Alexander Column, 704 tons of granite commemorating Russian victories over Napoleon. It is a space designed for spectacles, for the movements of people in crowds, for the shifting of clouds overhead. Walking across the square in mottled sunlight, a single person becomes more than a person.

Opposite page: View of the Neva with a spire, from the Cathedral of St. Peter and St. Paul inside the Peter-Paul Fortress.

The person would reappear, languid—he was said to be an esteemed and assertive mathematician but the problem of being a person seemed to have exhausted him, seated some distance away, whispering with Rosa, but somehow simultaneously he was already also outside on the quiet street where a small crowd of intellectuals hung around gossiping, stooped because of his height, accepting a cigarette—as a theme, troubled—I had been told some months earlier that many people in a Russian audience will not understand the Western notion of subjectivity—which he agreed to translate. "I know in Russian you have no word for 'self' except as a passive suffix or a reflexive pronoun," I said, but he shrugged his shoulders and wouldn't talk about it. Subjectivity is not the basis for being a Russian person. Our independent separate singularity can hardly be spoken of, but, Arkadii said, "many people wish it." "You know," I said, "many of *us* wish to overcome it. We think that if we can surpass or supersede the individual self we can achieve a community." Our ideas are to some extent rooted in our Protestant past, and Russian, even Soviet, ideas are rooted in Russian Orthodoxy. A Protestant person stands entirely alone speaking to God. "Protestants," said Arkadii, "go to church to mail a letter to God, the church, it's like a post office. The Orthodox church—the building is not symbolic—it is considered to be the real body of God, and Orthodox people too are God because they are together there, not alone, and speaking, by the way, has nothing to do with it." We have our great, modern, inescapable but not universal theme of isolation and alienation. "Yes, I suppose so. You are afraid of your finitude, and we are afraid of our infinitude."

The old woman was brought from the back of the flat into her niece's room the way elf-people might coax a reluctant wizard from the depths of a cave, the laughing, buzzing swarm growing quiet as she entered, looking up, setting drinks aside, turning toward her until all that was audible (as though it had been her own voice) was the sound of the rain flooding the courtyard below. Even in the gardens of Gogol Park, the dominant theme was the weeds. One didn't stroll down Nevsky Prospekt, one jostled. Our plane touched down in Moscow to pick up Ozzy Osbourne and Mötley Crüe. The bathwater filled the tub, as dark as tea. Once she had been a dancer with the Kirov. Instinctively, you squint as you suck on the end of your cigarette, the air of the room blue with toxins. Instantly, without notice, the schedule changed. Nadezhda's "brother" cursed. Mosquitoes rose up out of the cellars at night. Even the person is *remont,* under reconstruction. Your husband is "in hospital" with a heart attack, his fate uncertain, and you are entertaining fourteen intellectuals from four nations in your room, but this doesn't mean you're not wild with anxiety. Barrett showed Zhdanov how to focus the camera and we all huddled together, squinting in the sun. I saw this bridge in a film once, covered with the dead. From the air, vast tracts of land articulated the geometry of planned farming. A city without suburbs. The restaurant is open but has no food. "My sons, my sons," Zina said, taking each of the fascist thugs lightly by the elbow, "this is not how we treat our guests." A spoonful of raspberry jam to sweeten the tea. We escaped back into the rain.

Because we are poets we feel we can articulate a surface of any experience, but this omnipotence had to be learned. The opening remarks at our international summer school on language, consciousness, and society exhorted the participants to be scientific; we were also wished "health, long life, and apologies for street repairs." Arkadii's anticipation would prove to the point: "Language is a world in itself of which we must admit great difficulties of understanding. In this way, poetic activity is directed toward the outer world." The Russian cult of verse is based on a certainty of its object we would have difficulty ourselves understanding; that certainty radiates outward in several directions—as both collective heroism and resilient ground of speculation. For Suren Zolyan, who delivered the first *doklad,* "Poetic speech has a modal character," a change in its object paradigm being nothing less than a change in our worldview. "We need a strict definition of necessity for our theory of possible worlds." It is hard to imagine what this necessity will be for those who are even farther from materialism than we are (how readily material explanations are offered by Dan Rather, and we accept them in a sort of statistical blackmail); perhaps the poem's necessity for them has replaced a materialization that can only hurt. But even so for the Russians the poem is some kind of *object*—a concept very unlike the rich and theatrical demonstrations of intensity and loss we witnessed in its spontaneous delivery. The unity of two projects—call them scientific and cultural—around the poetic adds up to a kind of myth of the object whose authority ultimately lies in a transcendent inherence. And we were participants in this transcendence's social acting out, where somewhere from fifty to two hundred persons at any one time became its collective body.

Because we retain images of the present, the past takes on the appearance of a given experience. This makes us feel omnipotent, even though in the interval since taking the photograph events have changed its meaning.

The statue is of Lenin standing on a small, armored car, his finger pointing upward while he looks out, over the people. In the foreground is a bench, covered in flowers left there by couples on their wedding day. These floral offerings affirm that as one is wedded to another, one repeats a social troth as well. We can only articulate one surface of a given experience, which is why we misunderstand a poetry composed by a community seeking not to become an object. It makes a kind of myth of the "subject" whose gesture is iconic while the flowers are a testament of faith only two can share.

I left the others and took the bus back to the hotel. Upon arriving at the Finland Station, I walked in the direction of the river. It was satisfying to have mastered the transportation system and to realize that one could get around by oneself. That was when I spotted the statue and stopped to take a picture.

Opposite page: Arkadii Dragomoshchenko responding to a toast during a brunch for conference participants at the House of Friendship. Left to right: Aleksei Adashevsky, Soviet Cultural Foundation arts administrator; Valerii Zayayev, Leningrad painter; Alla Borisovna Pirskaya, an official with the Soviet Cultural Foundation; Dragomoshchenko; Barrett Watten; Ron Silliman.

The evening poetry reading was later moved, because of the crowd, to the auditorium where the day's talks had taken place, but it began in what must have been the parlor of the domestic quarters at the front of the building on Gertsena (or Herzen) Street, one flight above the street and ten feet from Nabokov's bedroom windows—but this fact was impossible to experience. The heavy, floor-length, faded rose curtains were drawn to close out the late-night daylight, the shadow of a tree, the smell of the mud in the trenches dug into the torn-up street, and the sound of the rain. Ivan Zhdanov, Nadezhda Kondakova, and Vyacheslav Ivanov (not the symbolist poet but the hero linguist and People's Deputy) recited their poems—they were far from the page—the poems committed to memory, we would say, but the impression was not that the poems lay in the poet but rather that they were exterior forms, materially musical, iambic and assonant, which each poet now spotted. Then Arkadii Dragomoshchenko pulled up a small table and sat down with his papers to read:

The future slams its door, always appearing before the mind
either as rubbish burning greasily and framed
by strontium-yellow ice
or as an a priori stone in the delectable flourishing of forms

for example, and

If this writes
I am not those who

and one of the young poets from Siberia stood to explain to Arkadii that he hadn't read poetry. Later, walking along the Neva across from the battleship *Aurora,* Aleksei Parshchikov agreed. "Why not?" Poetry is something completely expectable to a Russian. "Everybody looks for transcendence, and for that instead of religion for seventy-two years we've had poetry," said Sergei Timofeyev. "Now they are getting religion back, so what will happen in poetry?" "All these years," Parshchikov told me, "we've had a laugh, looking at the statue of Lenin where he's standing outside Finland Station. Do you see where he's pointing? Right at the KGB building."

Things appear out of order in a new environment—implies first *things,* and then *order.* Wordlessly, the driver of the black Volga ran the small sedan up onto the center island of the street, then off again, pedestrians scurrying like startled pigeons. An army with nothing to do, nowhere to go. To be on the seventh floor of the Hotel Leningrad was to be suspended over the city. On day five, I see my first jogger. The child on the elevator makes us an offer.

The woman reads my telegram back to me word for word. Suddenly, in front of the Dutch masters, I was surrounded by a tour group of floor-covering retailers from Northern California, their noisy American chatter the most alien thing I had ever heard. I ate the bowl of ice cream, or what I hoped was ice cream. In the gallery was an oil painting of a baseball game—the infield black, as if made of asphalt. The person reaches out to toast the strangers. At the opening of the conference, Arkadii repeats my comment on the circus, "clowns and wild animals," as a model for this event. Viktor Mazin points at my text: "What do you mean by 'Manson Family,' is that a TV show?" The river would reappear, languid.

Does poetry have any knowledge, and if so, what? In the West at times one feels as if the blank space of the poetic were a cult object to quantify the unknown. Knowing anything—or more important *not* knowing anything—in terms of poetry enters one into larger questions of the possibility of the world, and it may be that many who pass through poetry, but do not remain with it, do so for that reason. The poetic at the start of a successful business career, for example, might at best be an exercise in the negated modality of language. How would we know if the Russians saw their verse practice in any other way? If the poetic creates new meaning, what kind of meaning must be in place for that to be true? For one poet, "Poetic expression is the rebirth of context"—assuming it had been there all along; *in* the poetic it is reborn. And then I heard, "Fate is like a blind camel breaking down the man." Osip Mandelstam is a quote: "What I am saying is not me saying it"—it speaks *through* him. For another, it is "as if certain formal characteristics could be translated from our states of mind." Some of these would be identical to "ancient Russian idioms," making all modern Russians contiguous in some inner way. Yet another wants "to go through grammar to reach other levels of language" and imagines that "each person has his own language rules." "Futurist art," therefore, "has its own dominant in consciousness." I marvel at this form of belief. There are some people, evidently, for whom "every thought is a kind of process like light," or who at least can imagine those words enough to speak them. "Above socialism would be a new form of technical reality identical to language," another says. "I will attempt to describe this process from the point of view of linguistic use." But for us increasingly the poetic can only be known as its history. First we were displaced by it, and then we reasoned why. After that, we had knowledge.

But Petersburg is not merely imaginary; it can be located on maps—in the shape of concentric circles and a black dot in the middle; and this mathematical dot, which has no defined measurement, proclaims energetically that it exists: From this dot comes the impetuous surge of words which makes the pages of a book; and from this point circulars rapidly spread.

—Andrei Bely, St. Petersburg

Although, from this distance, it seems less a place than a series of conversations. And much happens in subsequent months to alter the meaning of that place.

The card reads "Dmitrii Prigov, Poet, Artist," and his address is written in roman characters, as though for Western export. He hands it to me in Gertsena Street, in front of the Composers Union where we are meeting. The street is torn up for sewer or water repairs, the rubble becoming a metaphor for much that happens during the week. It also stands for a level of production (or lack thereof) that one sees everywhere—streets unpaved, buildings halfway completed, restoration

Opposite page: Art crowd. Liteinny Prospekt outside Ariadne's Gallery, an exhibition devoted to painting and sculpture by Soviet women artists and organized in conjunction with the Summer School.

projects stalled, electrical wires exposed, basements flooded. The infrastructure is old, the bureaucratic agency empowered to fix it seemingly older.

The card is part of an elaborate potlatch of books, scraps of paper, addresses, and small offerings exchanged throughout the week. They are signs of community, in many cases, among total strangers. The press prefers to describe the period as a "thaw," hedging bets against an inevitable retrenchment. We participate in this change of weather (it is actually rather warm and sultry this day) simply by being in this street, gingerly stepping over the trenches and potholes on our way into the Composers Union. Before entering, Prigov gives me a small packet, stapled on all sides, containing, he says, fragments of his poems torn into tiny confetti.

If a poem is a repository of knowledge, then a form of the poem would be a head. But Prigov calls the confettied poems in packets "Coffins," a title that was funny previously and that may now be ironic. The question is who tore the poems, and that is a question of context. If the state tore up the poems, the cultural context is one in which poetry represents a challenge and a conflicting picture of power. If the people tore the poems, the cultural context has turned poetry into litter. "It sounds as if you're nostalgic for the years of oppression," I said to Viktor Lapitsky, really meaning only to tease him. "Maybe so.

Why not?" he said. "Then everything was important. Now everything means nothing. So you see, in a few short months we became postmodern," without transition. Earlier, I had disagreed with the sinologist, Vladimir Malyavin—or possibly misunderstood him—when he had said that postmodernism summons up the world in an Eastern spirit, that is, *consciously,* despite the long European tradition which has assumed the world *unconsciously.* But it was dizzying trying to think of the context for meaning, and therefore the context for knowledge (and I'm convinced that poetry participates in the processes of knowing), among people who are simultaneously Eastern and Western without resolution, without boundaries, at least not as I feel them. The given that traditionally is a poem would be embodied formally, not thematically. The poem is a weaving out of air, not of things. I wonder what the world is that is demanded by postmodern Russia.

The memory slices directly into the center of the chest. Does poetry have knowledge, and if so, how? I noticed you first talking in the cellar with Prigov and Kutik, squinting as you inhaled on an Opal. Later, in Castro Valley, over the car radio, Codrescu stammers through his childhood hometown, tape recorder in hand. The name *Hejinian* would be a form of risk in Baku. The produce glows, radiant, under the mist and lights in Safeway. In

Frankfurt, there's a porn arcade right in the airport—large rubber doll in black lingerie. At night, the basement of the Hotel Leningrad becomes a disco. They don't need trash cans on the street because who would throw anything away? What Mandelstam saw written on Hannah's forehead. Between *stul* and *stol*, to construct a discourse. How is this different from D. M. Thomas's version of the tale? I recall the colors, pastels dissolving into gray, the sky grayest of all. The mass was held in Croatian. We sprinted up one flight of stairs, then down another, then changed our minds, scrambling even faster back, then changed our minds again, only to wait an hour for the next train to the airport, and from there into a cab to the hotel. The head of Lenin emerged on the conveyor belt. Originally, the street had housed bankers and jewelers to the tsars. My ability to name an emotion does not tell me how to respond. Prefab wooden boxes, stacked three stories high at the edge of the park, to house the workers who will "fix" the hotel. He looks Italian and his name's Jamal. "I'm a victory baby," laughed Arkadii, as I am also. Tarn says that to imagine a community in poetry is preposterous. Only knowledge could find the luggage. In Michael's photo, there is only one pigeon on the head of Mayakovsky, whereas in mine (taken just seconds later) there are two. Arkadii puts Lyn and me into the first car—the driver's just a private citizen who owns a tattered vehicle, a spiderweb of cracks occluding its windshield—while he follows with Barrett and Michael. The plan of the hotel is exceedingly simple, one corridor per floor. (It was here, in one of the tea shops alongside the stairwell, where I had my first meal, rock-hard bread and rusting mineral water, while Misha called to find out that his wife had given birth.) Billiard balls were as large as the people. *Roan* is how you pronounce my name. Placing a phone call is like making a bet: the odds are against you. The trains don't pass through Leningrad Station—they come, literally, to the end of the line. Nabokov's house is empty. "This is the last tomato you will see for ten days," she said, as we headed unknowing into the sea of tomatoes.

To begin with, the specificity of the person who responded to Mikhail Dziubenko: "You are connecting information and language, but it's not so." Dziubenko agreed: "Connecting language to information reduces it somehow; deep layers of language are reduced. Information can be understood either in its discrete form—a row of signs on display—or as a continual process—the never-ending process of making sense of information, just as internal speech is continuous." Basing his analogies on the linguistic archaeological tropes of Spivak's cultural dominants in consciousness, Dziubenko finds language now functioning in terms of economic laws. One could equally penetrate the vertical layers of language, going down one hundred years, or move horizontally into a society of information (the general view of what the Americans have now). The phase difference of this process from one social continuum to another would be, as I understand it, what informs our critique under the conference's rubric, "language, consciousness, and society." It seemed at times a debate encased in its own parameters, an island in time discontinuous from the world adjacent to it on the street. That, too, could be a part of its critique. "All information is appropriation," according to Dziubenko, but in the making sense of it "a man can own his own language," to quote Marx. Then the abolition of private property would be exactly our appropriation of the sense of language once made and hence owned? I suppose the Russians have inherited this notion of the public—in what precise form?—from the methodology of the state. Thus by virtue of their method's proceeding from "outside," language must always be understood as unstable—"Language is like a harmonic complex, reflecting all the movement that exists in the world." Our form of the state makes language the site of contradiction, to which we return by means of our methods; for us language appears to be something still remaining to be *built.* Hence the futile attempts at ironic transcendence that drift through our poetry, reflecting a social space comprised of a series of imposed ironic norms. But according to the next speaker, "The law is inside the apple, and the target is Newton's head." The specificity of the person who responded, "Your method is terrible. You want to locate material intention in the author, whereas the reader is what counts." Later, he defended the elision, in my talk, of the artist's intention from the meaning of Tony Smith's cubes—the possibility of which could have meant *what* to him?

From over my shoulder Katya translated the lecture, word for word, in a whisper. It was difficult figuring out a possible context for words so divorced from their syntax, and so I would tune out, listen to the cadences of the speech or imagine what was being said, based upon responses from the audience. If they laughed, I laughed too. Barrett was taking notes at a furious pace, and so I didn't worry about not understanding everything—I could read later what I didn't understand now.

Later someone raised the question of postmodernism in the West. He argued that most debate depends on a high level of technological expertise—access to computers, software, televisions, and telecommunications equipment. Thus the romance of computer hackers breaking into multinational or defense networks as a form of subversion seems an irrelevant issue in—for example—Poland.

At times I tune in to what Katya is saying and write in my notebook as if to imitate a certain diligence I notice being practiced by my colleagues. I write, therefore I comprehend. I write: "The heat in the Composers Union is becoming unbearable. Why doesn't someone open a window? Which of the bald-headed composers in the hall outside is Prokofiev? Is Lyn's illness a product of last night's dinner, and if so, do

Opposite page: Vyacheslav Vasilievich Ivanov, Moscow semiotician and philologist, deputy to the All Peoples Congress.

I feel nauseous? What in the water supply might cause one's teeth to become black?"

A Polish intellectual introduces his remarks by saying that he represents theory whereas his friend "does the politics." I was not present for his talk, but these remarks were repeated to me, as someone asserted, verbatim. The knowledge that poetry "has" must be measured in terms of the transmission system available at that time—including the question of what time we are talking about and what measures it. There must be other questions this conference is raising outside of the quotation marks around "language, consciousness, society," but will I remember them?

It wasn't the food and it wasn't neurasthenia. The French were right in saying that the conference was more a dialogue between Russians and Americans than something more widely international, but that didn't increase the stability of our immediate experiences of "language" and "society" and "consciousness." To achieve a passage between Russian and American experiences, one negotiates vast fields of vertiginous shimmering. By that sixth day I felt enervated and motion sick from so much shimmering—and from absorbing so much disintegration. In the afternoon I dreamed that I was in a rural hotel in a village near Leningrad where other hotel guests have seen ghosts. The ghosts are becoming more violent at every sighting, and now several have taken a child and have thrown it against the wall. I begin to pack quickly to get away and save my little daughter who is with me and whose name is Mira Rabotnaya—bad Russian for "Worker's World." Arkadii came to the room with a jar of plain rice that Zina had sent, and by six o'clock I was fine again—hanging out at the hotel hard-currency bar and talking to Viktor Lapitsky about Gogol's literal necrophilia and his obsessive fear of being buried alive. They say that, sometime after his death, Gogol's body was exhumed, and they found the corpse twisted in the coffin. Zina told an anecdote that was circulating about an event that had happened on Vasilii Island, where Malii Prospekt and Shevchenko Street intersect. A little girl was apparently playing on the trolley tracks near the switching rails. The rails switched and seized her foot and she couldn't pull it free. A colonel was going by and ran over to help her; he was trying but he couldn't get her foot out from between the rails. Suddenly from behind her he saw a trolley coming around the corner—he was fighting to free the little girl's foot—then at the last minute he pulled off his greatcoat and threw it over the child's head, to spare her the sight of the instrument of her death.

The image of the gold spire shimmering, reversed in the water. The implosion begins. I could not explain how, in the Senior Professional Baseball League, one team traded Luis Tiant for five hundred stuffed teddy bears. The man stares at the photograph in the small blue passport, then up at me, then back at the passport again. Years ago, Rossi-Landi understood semiotics as the application of metaphor to a social field—that the metaphor was always language was a happy coincidence—and so reversed directions, using economics as the metaphor through which to look at language. To proceed through Nevsky Prospekt is to walk through modernism. The smell of mildew at the bottom gave no indication, as we climbed this dark stairway, of the sumptuous apartment that would unfold before us beyond Dmitrii's door, its small rooms made larger by many antique mirrors. The old woman toasted us silently the way one would soldiers from an invading army. Where did the Russians get redwood before it came from Vietnam? How does the woman selling tampons from a card table outside the Hermitage differ from the man selling dark glasses and back issues of *Honcho* from a blanket on the sidewalk of Second Avenue? On the television, Nelson Mandela is an old man, describing calmly how a colleague—a university lecturer—had been buried up to his neck in the earth of the prison, simply left in the sun until he screamed for water, at which point the guards urinated into his face. On the television, I watch the dead falling in the snow on this same bridge on which I now stand and wonder if boats passed down the Neva that winter, and, if so, what became of the corpses as the bridges were raised at one in the morning? In the piano room, prodded by Oleg, Sasha reluctantly shows us his visual poems, small sheets of collaged construction paper with texts that, read aloud in a theatrical baritone mixed oddly with a shyness that is almost painful, shine with assurance. Ostap sits in the back of the theater with his friends, observing the poets of his father's generation, some meeting one another for the first time, with the perfect cynicism of youth. As a dancer in the Kirov, she had seen Lenin and he her. The only people who stop to wonder at the train encased in glass off to one side of the platform must be tourists. Even though the hard-currency shop was empty, neither of the two clerks made the slightest motion toward me until I turned to ask for their help. I left the funeral and drove over the bridge in the torrential rain out to the Marin headlands, repeatedly stopping to ask directions, once even from a couple whom I found living beneath an abandoned building by a small lagoon, until I arrived at the conference center, discovering that the other group there that weekend consisted of scientists and environmental artists from the Leningrad Writers Union, there to discuss how best to save the Neva (asked if he knew Adashevsky or Dragomoshchenko, the geologist shook his head: "They're poetry, we're prose"). Articulate now the things I did not do. I stand next to the giant eight ball, air and sky a deep, brilliant red. Gradually, Michael and I learn the trick of turning the key, then pulling the door before pushing it to get into our room. I never set foot upon the *Aurora.* Aleksei turns to the driver. Next month, Ilya Kutik will read his poems, "in Russian and in translation." Dear Ostap, the medal you gave me has now been passed on by the person to whom I in turn gave it, your conditions still intact. Rosa Televisor at the back of the bus. A small man, waving beside his own statue of Pushkin. Imagine a language with no present tense. Having no other way to spend my rubles, I had the hotel staff launder my clothes daily. Now, at the end of her life, she will witness the end of the Revolution also. This store for milk, that for bread, but the kiosk sold tiny summer apples. Where time has been reversed, anything could happen next. Sunbathers leaning on the fortress wall. Where is Enver's poem? I don't think we're in Leningrad anymore, Toto.

Imagine a language with only a past tense. It is now only six months after our return from Leningrad. Driving from the memorial service, I found myself in the car alone on a freeway in California in early February, clouds having broken up from a morning rain soon to regather for more. I think of Tarkovsky's clouds in *Solaris,* an immediate absence where the figments of consciousness at once so present could not be attested to. "They are only clouds." The clouds in Dovzhenko's *Aerograd,* enormous counterpoint to puny biplanes plying their historic mission to the new Soviet Far East, become the impalpable evanescent background into which all such forward material incursions dissolve. I had not felt such a quality of being alone since Leningrad. My time was spent there in marking a notational system for a poetics of loss. What had happened to the future tense? Is it dissolving in fragments due to evanescent incursions of information from the West? Had we been ordered as replacements for Dovzhenko's biplanes? Even my mother had been involved in the exchange, organizing an exhibition of Soviet painters with a Russian émigré businessman from Walnut Creek—the paintings conveying a particular naïveté my mother couldn't read but instinctively knew she liked. It was odd to see their subjective utopias hung in identical frames in the mezzanine of a downtown office building in Oakland (just as odd as it is to see our subjective utopias in identical frames in this prose). I was seeing myself against the background of only myself—that was the absence of *you.* And then I wrote—more disjunct phrases to fill up a notebook. Ivanov had met Tarkovsky and spoke with him about the problem of filming a dream: "Dreams in the cinema have to be as clear as what in the cinema are not dreams." This is because "the film director makes all the things that death makes of life—the way death makes sense of it." I dream that I live in a communal flat called "The Poetry Project" with Carla and Asa and many others. For the next speaker, Abram Yusfin, "the form of a work of art is a kind of hologram, and all these holograms organize a mathematical space. This explains how different artists of different epochs might meet in their creativity while they have never met each other." (George Lakoff on the phone momentarily interrupts this.) "We need to find these holograms. *Community* is what we are dealing with, not one man or one work of art." And then Yulia Latinina stands forth: "The Stalinist epoch could not admit to an abstract person. We must realize those mechanisms that build a man." One of her folkloric examples: "The axe is floating in the river/And my sweet man is building the Volga Don Channel!" When Anya was interrupted by a man who didn't like her translating out loud for me, she said (with objective rigor), "Ya rabotayu" (I'm working). According to Vadim Baronov, "Every text has the feature of a double objectivity. It is not only the object of a universal space but the object of our speech. This double objectivity can be overcome and united into one in speech." (This noise outside the window interferes.) (Playing chess in a dream, the machine always wins.)

2

In August the surface of the Moika, like that of the Fontanka, was darker and smoother than the surface of the Neva. The gray-green waters of the Moika and Fontanka slid along their embankments under wrought-iron bridges, but the waters of the Neva were hidden below the river's pale silver surface, a surface of light on which smooth or sharp shards of yellow, blue, and white brighter broken light rose, turned, floated by, sank, and reappeared, light expanding on the river and evaporating into the city, illuminating it with mist. In this not quite solid landscape (with which the intense solidity of interiors contrasts so dramatically) there is no vanishing point, unless it is oneself. But there is a certain point—I was shown many such points—at which demolition and construction achieve stasis, with a heap of building materials on the ground, mud, rotting planks in the mud, rubble, and it is at these points that the project comes to rest. "This is why Russia is not a great military strength," I was told, "because the soldiers settle in the rubble and discuss beauty, which is somewhere out of the ugliness off in the mist." Real things in the city's mitigated spaces (conditioned by vapor more of light than of water) seemed distant and indistinct; buildings, trucks, bridges existed as if lost in space, but the very same light which seemed to dematerialize objects

Opposite page: Fontanka River.

saturated certain colors: reds of a deep organic darkness and substantiality, and blues, greens, and yellows, pastel but unfaded, not pale, of an almost emotional intensity, so that these colors were, in themselves, beautiful.

My first visual image of the social space of Leningrad was split between horizontal and vertical registers. Crowds of people, untold numbers similarly dressed in light colors, summer clothes, were arrayed in both directions on the street parallel to our movement into the city and away into intersecting streets one after the other. Abrupt buildings with an absolute five- or six-story limit, dark and encrusted with architectural ornament from more modern periods in the rebuilt sectors, make solid walls to contain the microdynamics of movement between and within. "Leningrad: Geroi Gorod," hero city, is in large letters above a public square, scaffolding behind them evident. In the PBS documentary of the Leningrad siege, the central parts of the city looked virtually identical to the way they look today (they have been rebuilt, as the Germans methodically shelled them sector by sector). After that history which everyone remembers and no one wants to admit, it is still, as Arkadii says, like it was in the fifties—nothing has changed. Because people want it that way? Men with their war medals on streets and buses are in their sixties; on the Moscow road, the late-Stalinist attempt at relocating the urban center out of the old city failed, although the somewhat larger apartments in its pre-postmodern baroque are valued for their conveniences. The large windows of lavish artists' studios for union members in one apartment building make a political comment, but there were few exhortations to labor except at ugly intersections in the outskirts. Generally, there is a feeling of time having stopped, like the three hours in the siege when the metronome broadcast over the public address system wound down because people were too weak to wind it. The city seems just to have recovered from the period of mourning for those events. Ten thousand people died a day. Olga Khrustalyeva's grandmother was born in 1904 and lived through the siege; when she came out of her room in the family apartment to meet the foreigners, we gave her a serious toast. That was something like looking at Leningrad.

It would be a door onto Europe, a new city rising, quite literally, from the mud. Neva: the Mud River. Hence the names one associates with its construction—Rastrelli, Falconet, Le Blond—are more than architects and designers; they are signs of an empire without that would legitimize the empire within. Unlike Moscow, Leningrad begins at a definite moment: 1703. The "old" city is, by European standards, the "new" city, each square reflecting the aspirations of *l'ancien régime,* but on a considerably larger scale. When the "newer" regime takes over in 1917, it inhabits the frame of the old, transforming churches, statues, and thoroughfares into monuments to the Revolution. The Kazan Cathedral, with its vast arc of Corinthian columns, now houses the Museum of Atheism. Leningrad was once Petersburg. Like layers of an onion or like the expanding crescents of canals, Leningrad's history moves outward from the eighteenth century. At its base is the river.

In my photo of Lenin's closed train, now encased in glass at the Finland Station, one can see a group of women wearing brightly colored flowered dresses. I was afraid of taking their picture directly and so used the glass as a convenient mirror.

"Cock dyela" crows the rooster striding over the gravel between the blue palace and the pond, beyond which a string quartet's tones are amplified and so fill the air, here where once the Nazis waited for the day when they would enter Leningrad. A carriage house atop a flight of stairs—of course. Zhdanov stares at the bust of Plutarch. Nadezhda's "brother" growls. Arkadii says that every foreigner wants to have his/her photograph taken in front of the KGB building: its boring fifties-style architecture (it was in fact constructed in the 1970s) reminiscent of the sort of building that in the U.S. would be reserved for telephone equipment. We used scraps of wood from a nearby construction project as planks to cross the muddy exposed innards of Ulitsa Gertsena (Herzen Street). All these young Asian faces (races I've never even seen before, except in books), brilliant half-toothless smiles, belong to soldiers. Many of the doorways open sideways to the street, leading in to a second doorway, a means of keeping winter at bay. Finger-size potato pancake. The line for tickets to the Hermitage is nowhere near its entrance. Viktor shows me the publication, my own work in *samizdat,* an "American issue," myself sandwiched between Zukofsky and Woody Allen (a context in which I'm "the tall one"). At the back of the church stood tourists, aiming their cameras now at the young couple in the process of being married. Will she carry her bouquet out to the Bronze Horseman?

"When I say, 'I'm here now,' I utter an eternal verity, and when I say, 'Now I'm there,' I have uttered an eternal nonverity." Or so Katya explained, apologizing for what was not translation but interpretation. "I cannot read such texts because I must, you will excuse me, be my own text." Every statement can change a context and every context can change a statement. We are in the second, smaller of the two crowded and smoke-filled damp close cobalt-blue windowless basement rooms constituting the Composers Union café, smelling of meat, plaster, humidity, and cognac. It is hard to realize, and impossible to say, that I "had to remind myself" of something that was happening at that very moment. "But I think that he said that poetry has no operative opposite." It was the second or third day of the conference, and so August 10 or 11, and midafternoon. Zina slipped an apple into my hand and took a cigarette from Vitya's pocket—he was retranslating some papers. As Zolyan had said, "Fate is a blind camera malfunctioning in the wind." Or perhaps Katya had said that he had said "mind," noting his Armenian accent. It was later in the little Georgian café that we were hassled by the drunk anti-Semites, who were poking at Parshchikov, who looks strikingly like Pushkin, while insisting to us that the "good guys are north guys with blue eyes." Then

Opposite page: Aleksei Parshchikov, Moscow poet.

Zina appeared and walked them away. "My little sons," she told me she told them, "you and I, we understand all things about our Soviet problems, but these Americans, they don't understand. Let's let them eat and worry about their own problems, little sons."

Studying up for Russia, I went to see *Little Vera.* The family drama is framed by long opening and closing shots of their industrial town. Somewhere in the middle there is a slag heap of enormous proportions near which the people go to swim. Sergei: "What is your goal?" Vera: "I am going to communism." These vistas are what we have accomplished, each seems to say, and all that we have accomplished is loss. How could it appear otherwise to anyone from the outside world? From the vantage of our windows at the Hotel Leningrad, the classical finality of the city was confirmed in a vista of industrial haze. Production is only loss. On the streets where there are few signs, none of the conventional markers divide the economy among its parts—there are only numbered doors the people disappear into and issue from. How long living in Leningrad would it take for such a perception to change? Looking out from the Supreme Soviet-styled dining arena at the hotel, Katya mentioned that she had been born in sight of the same view of the Neva, but that her family's apartment had been torn down not to make way for the modern hotel but so that its guests would not have to trouble themselves with overlooking any everyday life. What remains around the world-class hotel are a vacant lot, an abandoned group of apartments still waiting to be torn down on Prospekt Karla Marksa, an anomalous modern building in baby-blue tile, and a rundown military hospital with guards at its entrances. Around the corner we are in another world, out of sight of any organizing perspective, and dissolving into a pointillist economy. For what I think of now as political reasons I have always been attracted to the empty spaces between things; I would like to make a rhetoric of them to prove an historical truth. Russia would give me more than enough opportunities to do so. Then the station of the metro approaches us, and we descend into its pneumatic tube. Lights are strung out at even intervals along our diagonal movement downward. In some of the stations enormous metal doors separate the people from trains.

4

The questions came up often: What is value where there is so little to exchange; what is money when there is little to buy; what does money become after the Revolution?

We gathered in Dmitrii Spivak's sitting room with its plush furniture, leather-bound books, red-textured wallpaper, somewhat exhausted from the day's events. It was late, we had had no dinner, and as far as we knew, there was only to be "a little apple cake" and tea. As pleasant as this sounded, it would clearly not be enough to feed the fifteen of us who had convened in this rather elegant apartment. Everyone seemed subdued and a little irritable—except Dmitrii whose boundless enthusiasm was tempered by impeccable good manners. On one wall of the room was what looked to be a Chagall drawing of a woman who seemed to be floating in an indeterminate space. Dmitrii explained that it was indeed a Chagall and that it had been given to his mother long ago by the artist, with a personal inscription penned on the back. The drawing had then been given to Dmitrii as a birthday present when he was a boy. He was extremely fond of the drawing (although it was a schematic rendering, typical of Chagall, the woman's ample breasts and seductive eyes dominated the design) and wanted to hang it over his bed. He found a handsome oval frame and, in order to accommodate the rectangular drawing to the circular format, cut the drawing to fit, thus eliminating the handwritten *dedicace* and painter's authenticating autograph. "It was the most expensive mistake I have ever made," he said ruefully. "But at least I had *her* over my bed."

At the end of his story, we all sat down at a large round table where we were served plates of cold cuts, cheese, crudités, cauliflower with white sauce, tomatoes, and spectacular pizza, all the while drinking excellent Georgian white wines and vodka. The conversation became animated, and the festive mood gained momentum when Dmitrii delivered generous toasts in four of the many languages he knows. We finished, as promised, with an excellent apple cake and tea.

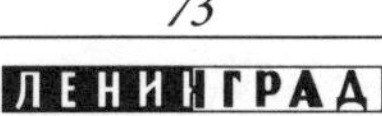

In *Alexander Nevsky,* two hardy soldiers (one blond in a way that to a Soviet audience would be "totally Leningrad" almost as, in the U.S., Woody Allen would be "totally New York") vie for the hand of a young woman. The bad guys in the wonderful helmets sink beneath the ice.

"Your conference is all the news," says Spivak, "that and the earthquake in San Francisco." At the consulate, electricians were rooting around in an exposed wall, perhaps searching for bugs. She is blonde allright, but small, and wiry to the point of anorexia. The ice over the Ladoga proved so sturdy that they were able to build roads across it, sending out the women and children in caravans of trucks each winter, the vehicles returning with food for those who remained. I repressed the impulse to reach forward and touch Nevsky's helmet. To construct a nation was the ultimate modernist project. Hocquard worked hard to achieve his small scandal, but the context was so different that the act itself lost even the force of its rudeness. Each city will have its circus. Barrett's voice carried those familiar clear tones over the staccato of hammers and saws in the middle of the night. Lightning demonstrated the scope of the sky. I repressed the impulse to reach forward and touch your face. The man who passed (a playwright) immediately consented to serve as our translator. Instead of coins, I received my change in small candies. The sumptuousness of breakfast at the hotel for foreigners marked each bleak meal that would follow that day. Even the department store was closed for repairs. "During the summer, I work for my father," said James Kenney's daughter in her office at the consulate. In the Georgian lunchroom, giant beakers of flavored sugar water were hung upside down in a rack on the counter, like giant hummingbird feeders. How do you "butter" parsley? A one-size-fits-all drain plug from Rubbermaid. Carefully pouring the Pepsi into our glasses like a fine wine. During the fighting, the rough blonde one discovers a second female, herself a sturdy woman, capable in battle—thus harmony (monogamy) is restored to the world.

Of the five currencies, I had three: ordinary rubles, European *valuta* (Finnish marks), and U.S. dollars. They were incompatible in most purchasing situations, and they forced me into different roles in certain social situations. The other two currencies I've never seen: the *valuta* ruble ("real Russian money," which only exists in principle but is fully operative) and an experimental ruble (according to rumor it is to be issued, but only in certain cities, as "international money" for use in transactions between the USSR and Eastern bloc nations; perhaps it doesn't exist at all, except in contemporary Soviet mythology). Opportunities to spend ordinary rubles were rare, and what was offered wasn't magnificent. I visited a cooperative store called "The Butterfly"—one of the new, *glasnost*-era "privately owned" shops—and saw two small chipped saucers displaying costume jewelry, one very expensive brittle leather motorcycle jacket which a grandmother was fingering, a rack of assorted dusty wool coats, one cotton washdress, some knick-knack animal figurines, a few basic kitchen implements including a saucepan—the goods offered and the aesthetics of presenting them were exactly like those of a very small St. Vincent's or Goodwill Store. In the hotel the main restaurant and the bar took only hard currency, but the buffet in a basement corner took rubles, and

Opposite page: People awaiting trains at Finland station. Barely discernible behind the glass in the background is the train that brought Lenin to St. Petersburg in February 1917.

there I could spend one every morning for breakfast, or four if I got to the woman at the desk where one prepaid the fixed price ahead of Barrett, or Ron, or Michael. Outside the hotel on the street, belligerent kids on the black market approached speaking English to ask if we were American and wanted to change money. *"Non, nous ne sommes pas—nous sommes français,"* I said to repel them, and they turned away. In this market the American dollar is the only currency with value—but it is almost not a currency, being pure, with value against nothing. It's the kids who have value. At a state-owned store called "The Birch," Western tourists can spend their hard currency. Everyone seemed to be finding it a great relief to do so, and four Italians and fifteen West Germans were spread out through the store alerting each other to available things while two Russian women sat at a counter translating the ruble price into its assigned German or Italian equivalent. I bought Zina an umbrella—umbrellas had disappeared several months earlier from the regular stores—and bottles of wine to take to Dmitrii's flat later. Ahead of me in the line waiting to get to the cash register, a German woman was balancing *matryoshka* dolls and long-handled lacquer spoons on a small matching yellow lacquer tray, looking frantically for a place to put her things so she could get to her *valuta,* and Arkadii was digging in my purse for mine. "Do you notice that there aren't so many things even here anymore? Pretty soon even the Westerners won't be able to buy things, and then everyone will go crazy together."

There are no suburbs in Leningrad but dissolving patches of urban space that yield to countryside. The five million people are simply piled on top of each other in the old city, addended by housing projects of various eras and styles. Monuments hold down the organizing conjunctions of major intersections with semantic weight. The spaces between the sixties concrete blocks where Arkadii and Zina have their apartment are filled, however, with northern birch forests in a seemingly natural, unimproved state. Diagonally through a gap in the trees old men playing chess can be descried from the fourth floor. The Bronze Horseman is a blind spot no one can see but for the wedding bouquets at its feet; the gold dome of the unclean St. Isaac's Cathedral in the background, under reconstruction, menaces and will not yield. Walking back toward the hotel along the Neva in early evening but in full light, I noticed a plaque commemorating the house of the ever-yielding General Kutuzov, "the genius of the Russian type." Arkadii spoke angrily of the arts of war and Russia's national failure to master them. In the absence of any noticeable industrial plan, Leningrad's production strictly must be itself. Blowups of the city's modern masters—Shostakovich, Prokofiev, Glazunov (?)—framed over the ornate wallpaper of the Composers Union, three doors away from the house where Nabokov was born. The experiment in utopian industrialism we passed in the cab is now a brick ruin of about the same period as Henry Ford's Model T plant.

The image of Lydia Ginzburg, eighty years old and barely able to walk, being carried over the rubble of the torn-up street in a kind of improvised palanquin to give her address to the conference, an event which never happened but which was anticipated each day. I received two Pushkin pens and was shown the apartments where Akhmatova, Shklovsky, and Joseph Brodsky lived. The enormous red tile image of Mayakovsky in the metro that bears his name; I spoke of his neologisms to blank disinterest and was corrected on my pronunciation of Pasternak: *Boris Leonidovich Pasternák.* Gigantic female slaves hold up an entrance to the Hermitage; we cannot remember what is depicted in the monument commemorating victory over the Germans in 1943. Adashevsky resolutely did *not* want us to visit the cemetery, so we walked through the meticulously restored Summer Palace in strapped-on felt sandals instead.

What replaces the object is what is said during a long lunch at the Architects Union or late drinks at Olga's apartment. After one such occasion, we were standing in the hallway, collecting our coats and umbrellas, when a door opened onto a sitting room to reveal another party in progress, a party that had obviously been going on throughout the evening as oblivious to us as we had been to it.

"I worry about these reforms," Malyavin had been saying earlier the same evening, "if by that one means the attempt to impose Western-style capitalism, *tout court.* It just won't work—and I fear that we would lose something much more important in the process." We had been talking nonstop, as near as I could figure it, since eight o'clock in the morning, and the evening was young.

What I took that I hadn't brought: a letter addressed to a computer firm handling software for Russian language instruction; two Russian stamps in payment for mailing an application to a conference on cybernetics; an envelope containing the fragments of a poem that had been torn into tiny pieces; an empty Kosmos cigarette package, white star on blue background; the address of a person to whom I would send the poems of Jim Morrison; an article translated from the Polish on pop culture in America; a packet of glossy postcards depicting monuments and buildings of Leningrad; the address of a person who wanted the complete works of Jacques Derrida; two kopeks.

I pasted stickers of nouns up on all the objects of my world. Did the "brother" stay behind to hold our coats and bags to keep the museum staff from stealing, or to search that which we never left in our rooms? I got off the bus near the Engineers Museum and simply walked the empty streets, still damp from the rain. The path to the apartment is through an inner courtyard, exactly as in Paris. I could sense Ilya's admiration—an acceptance that would have bordered on awe had it not been grounded solidly in his own life as poet—as he spoke of the role of Brodsky. As a young woman, Akhmatova had been anorexic and looked like an uptown version of Toklas. "We have no national identity," Malyavin said. "It's ridiculous—we're eleven peoples." Elaborate painted porcelain covers the tsar's wood stove. Of course, a high rise in the trees. The doors to the apartment tell you nothing about what awaits inside. On the street, poets gather between storms, oblivious to whomever is presenting the paper inside (Maxim Shapir drones on for hours), passing cigarettes back and forth, slow sweet intellectual schmoozing. Lyn stayed back at the hotel, sick from the tension or the water. When Katya began to speak of your husband ("What a character! Every night's a party!"), I felt anxious, distracted, depressed. It is impossible not to twitch with embarrassment at the dreadful writing in the film *Miss Firecracker*. Between two rooms of French Impressionists was a plywood corridor, a tunnel. Arkadii's body as he stood by the black cab under the lamp in the small airport parking lot reflected an energy that had surpassed all exhaustion. The ornate parquet floor composed of redwood forms a vast pattern (diamonds within stars, almost a sequence of snowflakes) that spreads out across the banquet hall, its walls an intricate sequence of beveled mirrors, the murals on the ceiling sectioned into rectangles as if a gallery of frescoes—yet outside the garden is filled with rough-edged nameless plants in the fractal array of accrued nature, the front gate in the same collapsing disrepair in which the Nazis left it forty-five years before.

"Goodbye, America, where I've never been; I will float forever in my paper boat." Arkadii was repeating in English the words to a song on the cassette in the red plastic tape deck. Although more than a few of the poets had expressed, at one time or another, humility and likewise irritation at their material circumstances (which included a long lack of access to such artistic materials as "ideas from the West," ideas which they assume surround us in our paradise of possessions), yet they say what we don't have is their light. And lacking that, we don't have their colors. It is equally the light and the language that characterize Dragomoshchenko's *description.* In the Bay Area, the light, despite and even in the fog, is bright, strong, and bounded; it separates and maintains objects, as if it were the source of their discreteness and their finitude, and makes the contrast between an object and its shadow definite and resolute. Meanwhile in Leningrad light and object merge; everything lifts in the light, drifts, is transformed, returns. The light comes from the side and is visible but diffuse, a mist in myriad tints. So Arkadii said that the blue of the sky is a shade of yellow. And while there is the shade called black, which glitters, another blue is a shade of black too, the black that doesn't glitter. Vitya, Olyessa, and Misha were laughing in Arkadii and Zina's kitchen, listening to the

Opposite page: Arkadii Dragomoshchenko reading at the conference.

cassette. "What he is saying," said Viktor Lapitsky, "is completely Egyptian." I wanted to know why the anti-Semites had listened to Zina, so Arkadii explained that she'd first asked them their age and then told them she was the mother of a son slightly older—"and even such boys slightly obey mothers." In the doorway Ostap had leaned several new paintings; on top was the one called *This Time We Are Both.*

The technology that will change the Soviet Union forever is Xerox, which is still unavailable for most. The meaning that has been built up over seven decades will not survive the paradigm shift of infinite copies. Where accessibility and power are the antinomies of everyday life, the irony of free information flow will radically undermine them. At the same time, the Russians have none of the redundancies on which we information gluttons thrive. There was no sense to the order of the symposium, for example, which seemed to change with every event, but somehow everyone got informed of it. Words have meaning when spoken in certain contexts; the natural inference is that the contexts will change. What if all contexts changed at once? Time is needed to build up the meaning of information we don't need. Who would ever want a universe of choice? What was in front of us at all times was a literal event. Power is the ability not simply to control information but to be the literal point where information issues forth. In this sense power operates in a virtually linguistic field. But what happens when the language is changed? A poetry embodied in memory becomes destabilized in its encounter with a poetry objectified in texts. Somehow there will be a union of the two, but epistemology will give out piteous groans at the unformed and chaosmic birth. Information, on our part, wants the confirmation of a literal time frame in the practical world. Reading my texts to the Russians, I felt through them the embodied impulse of a determining speech. The world I had made as the possibility of a text seemed to be inferred, in their temporal understanding, as coming into concrete existence as I read. Or so I may have imagined it, and I continued to imagine how I may have been, in writing, somehow continuous with the irony of unavailable power that inscribes the limits of their everyday life. What we have is certainly an opposite illusion; so much so that we accept even our own versions of ourselves.

> *Time is needed to build up the meaning of information we don't need.*
>
> —Barrett Watten

But it is by means of this information that we discover it is unnecessary. The dissemination of AIDS in the Soviet Union occurs primarily through transfusions; information about the disease is passed on by word of mouth. The absence of signage makes shopping difficult; the absence of objects makes signage meaningless. Not the power of information but the power in information is signaled by Bush's face on the hard currency bar television next to the chart of international exchange rates speaking, unexpectedly, in English. We affect nothing, really, but we talk as if we do, as if it is the last time to make a difference.

In order to announce the sequence of events at the conference, Barrett printed out the program on Arkadii's computer, over and over again. The copy of Tadeucz Rachwal's paper must have been the tenth or eleventh carbon impression; it was almost invisible, dealing, as it did, with the assimilation of postmodernism in Eastern Europe. Zhdanov glanced at the page, then lifted his eyes up, over the audience and began to recite from memory, the cadences rolling over us again and again. "A literal event," yes, but now attaining a dreamlike aura, that is, a reconstruction of time as a thing to be known. I still haven't got it right, the translator admitted.

Spell my name *POH*. Will I ever return? Here the grey-blue river creates neighborhoods: across the bridge is where the bureaucrats live. He'd been working as a dramaturge for a local theater group, very avant-garde, which was now able to function without censorship, meaning also that it now had to earn its own way, causing its director gradually to insist upon more and more standard, traditional fare. It's summer, therefore humid. If, suddenly, Japan were to sell microchips to the Soviet Union, the balance of the world would tip. I mix up a bottle of lemonade to hide the taste of the bacteria-killing chemicals in these little pills. On the edge of the Baltic, behind the monstrous apartment block, Arkadii waves his arms toward the horizon lost in the sunny haze: that way to Kronstadt, to Finland. The corridors of the Hermitage are *remont:* between the high-ceilinged exhibition rooms (I'm moving from Matisse to the Dutch), a tunnel has been built from plywood scraps, ill lit, as though the building were near collapse. I see the expression of pain in Viktor's face—the idea of independent presses disrupts a deeply held understanding of how to negotiate between *samizdat* editions (0-12 copies) and those sponsored by the state (ten thousand is the minimum run)—this new middle ground is like the spring thaw of the ice on the Ladoga, simultaneously dangerous and thrilling. The telephone operator insists that I can call America only at hours when no one will be at home. Back in Frankfurt I'm unable to sleep: as we leave the anonymous hotel tucked bizarrely behind some small factories along the sewage-choked tributary of the Rhine, something gets in my eye—I'm virtually blinded by the experience and Lyn leads me literally by the hand as we search the airport pharmacy for eye drops, then into the city by train, until suddenly, whatever it is washes away in Goethe's house. Olyessa Turkina is so quiet, so polite that it reinforces one's sense of her height, which is certainly less than five feet. "Language, Society, Consciousness"—which is the outer term? It's 1972 and Antoinette, Elliott's girlfriend (later his wife, then his widow), tells me that my poetry reminds her of these Russian linguists and critics she's been studying in school; she hands me a dittoed version of a paper by Shklovsky. Looking at the video of Goofy and Pluto, the Russians are no more able than ourselves to tell why one of these two dogs is anthropomorphized and the other not. At last the luggage arrives. The light in the basement café is impossible even to see by this late in the day—we sit in shadows speaking in languages we barely know. In rejecting the boy-next-door naval cadet (who will later return and attempt to rape her) for the insolent, worldly first-year college student, Vera ironically replicates the conflict between lovers in *Alexander Nevsky.* When I first meet Parshchikov and Zhdanov, I'm standing in Kit Robinson's backyard. There's no closure—only the rupture at the end of the text. After breakfast, I walk past the souvenir and newsstand on the mezzanine of the hotel, its one English-language paper a six-week-old edition of *People's World.* We're in what was once the home of a top tsarist military officer, now the headquarters of the Soviet Peace Foundation, where Arkadii is to meet Aleksei to discuss details, Adashevsky's committee meeting around a small card table in the corner of a sizable reading room while we wander into the banquet hall, giggling, goofing like teenagers at the ornateness of its long polished table, aping at our images in the mirrors, not realizing that three days later we will find ourselves in this same room at a formal luncheon held in our honor. The hostility between filmmakers from Leningrad and those from Moscow feels all too familiar. Without the legal capacity to use it to form businesses, money ceases to be capital. Visibly missing his daughter, Michael stares at every infant in a stroller on the street as we stroll back along the river (stunned at how many of these children have serious skin disorders). Visibly missing you, I send you this telegram.

3

Leningrad very pretty
and Leningradians are sweet
but the fruit of poor Lenin
is not enough to eat.

Later, the stylization of memory will crystallize around this light—the low flat pale sky glimmering off the Neva, the long palace a paler green, the shimmer of that one gold spire over the skyline. Later still, out the upper window of Goethe's house, I see Golf Haus across the narrow street. The iron taste of the mineral water clung to the roof of my mouth. For all its adolescent energy, Ostap's painting had a brooding quality (like the dark side of Philip Guston), muscular men in black against a rich red background, a giant eightball, light filtering in from the courtyard. Michael pulled the curtains back so we could watch the forks of lightning burst over the horizon. Deep red walls of a minor palace—but the curiously colorless buildings (by this I mean a dark grey) of Nevsky Prospekt. From the seashore we might see Finland. What I don't see is your luggage. Suddenly, atop the conveyor belt, there appeared a disembodied head. It's not the polio-twisted gait of Krivulin's that I would remember, but the fierce, psychotic look in his eyes. Because his wife had given birth just moments ago, he would not be permitted to see her for six days. Whole pitchers of kefir awaited us at breakfast, plates of shredded, pickled beets. Each key is anchored to a brown wooden ball, the room's number carved on top: this, when you leave, the humorless floor maid puts into a tray that she

Opposite page: Fontanka River.

keeps in a drawer of her desk (the TV at that station perpetually on, one talk show after another). Two pigeons asleep atop the skull of Mayakovsky. When I ask after your husband's health, I see panic flash across your blue eyes, and you don't even attempt an answer.

We are an object of attention that requires remembering. A flashbulb in a darkened room. Later, the interpretation of memory will give credence to this air, the flatness of a city in which gold domes catch the light. From this vantage we might look outward to Kronstadt from which soldiers fired or backward into the interior; it seems to stretch forever. We watch lightning from a vantage afforded few, ourselves the instance of its height. Inhospitable materials we recognize as our own. Meanwhile the city spreads in exfoliating circles, the faces of persons interrupting one's attempt to be one.

Lenin splits between state power and popular consent, and somehow the image of Lenin is supposed to account for both. In the city that bears his name, that image is the freeze-framed perfection of time in its development as being at the same time only retrospective. The train that took Lenin to the Finland Station is monumentalized under glass, such that taking a picture of it one obtains more the reflected image of crowds (the train station itself, as part of the military, is off limits for photographers). Military green railway cars with dark red stars move behind women with shapeless cotton dresses and shopping bags. The museum devoted to Lenin was *remont,* leading to the joke that Lenin too was *remont* for the foreseeable future. Without the image of Lenin there would have been no consent to the politics of Stalin; hence Lenin's absence leads to billowing waves of inchoate populism, with some fascism at the fringes. But without the image of Lenin there is still the state, those institutions that regulate the flow of the masses from their military trains. I too am split, between regulating my knowledge of the state with some dictum like "The state is a construction; Lenin was the architect of the state" and resenting the entombed memorials to Lenin's presence that still remain, only impediments to the restructuring at hand. Each morning the sun rose on the battleship *Aurora,* the obnoxious Christmas gift of an alcoholic uncle no one likes: a reminder of some tottering presence it would take violence to replace. It would even hurt you to do so, doing damage to a part of yourself: so the received idea of not having revolution without breaking eggs returns in its enormous cultural guilt complex. We identify with power we cannot change so as not to break any more eggs. Consent, which still exists, in this way becomes a form of neurosis; for this reason nonconsent can only take the form of extremes.

We can't identify ourselves with what is provoking unplaced (and thus seemingly baseless) passions because it isn't material. The immateriality is not a negation but an achievement, of independence from abstractions and from shortages, causing now, Arkadii writes, greater aggressiveness and numerous instances of panic. I remember referring—addressing my mother—to "my love affair with Russia," which she misunderstood as "my love affair with a Russian." The love object in the first case is immaterial (though real) and the emotion is, can I say?, exterior, like being in love with love, while in the latter case the love object would be material, physical, in response to an interior emotion. This exterior passion, or desire, for Russia is stirred by an insatiable identity. Being there is to be in a state of incommensurability, and hence of inseparability, as if that were the status or "human" nature of Not-me. Without anxiety, but with enormous sadness, I lost myself in the crowds flowing on the Nevsky.

When I saw, on the wall of their bathroom, two toilet-paper holders, each full, my first thought was "These people are flaunting it"—later, realizing that this was a communal flat, I understood that each family had its own roll, and wondered if they cheated and stole from one another. My identity is ascertained by a photograph in a small blue book. Brigada S used to be Brigada SS. The gold in your smile shines. Who I am is this pain in my chest, ungratified desire to weep. "No more surprises!" The cab driver (not a cab driver) suddenly lurches his vehicle forward down the unpaved, rubble-strewn street—he wants to buy our dollars, sell us cameras, film, do anything. Arkadii says of another, "He's a Soviet yuppie." Just ten weeks later, the ruble has been devalued by 90 percent. Here, take my insect repellent, please. A trio of giant cockroaches construct an anthology. "I was at Woodstock—they treat me as a goddess."

I too am split—between a temporal sequence (involving events received retrospectively and witnessed as if by a tourist looking at a diorama through glass) and a spatial field in which events seem to repeat themselves like so many columns in one of Rastrelli's colon-

Opposite page: Aleksei Adashevsky and, just behind him, Dmitrii Spivak, Leningrad linguist specializing in the linguistics of altered states.

nades. The diorama is the closed train, closed once again in glass and surrounded by the station that bears His name. The sequence of columns supports an edifice of state that at this very moment is being described as "crumbling" or "tottering." Cold War rhetoric is being dusted off to commend reforms taking place in Eastern Europe as having the "blessing" of Moscow. Young people dancing in the streets of West Berlin, crawling over the Wall, embracing each other in front of now-familiar graffiti, while we stare through the screen and the words of someone proclaiming the death of something.

The revolt at Kronstadt stands as the first of many islands in a historical topography that now includes El Salvador and Poland. These are rhetorical islands in the midst of unstable formations whose gestures of resistance have already been purchased and placed behind a protective shield. Later the stylization of memory will crystallize around this light.

Your boundaries are slipping: I imagine this is not the underlying message in the morality play of East meets West. According to Parshchikov, a Soviet citizen can travel anywhere in the Soviet Union without an internal passport. "You have a collective society, for whatever that's worth." Importing PCs will henceforth bring a tax of $20,000, roughly equivalent to their cash value on the black market. Russia is not a police state: no one seems to be in control. What it doesn't mean is that, on leaving Soviet airspace, the custom at least on Pan Am is to cheer. Three months later, outside Asa's school, I am accosted by two Russians trying to get to San Mateo who speak only Russian louder and louder at me until I will understand. Marianne's family hopes eventually to own their own accordion business. I tried to explain the politics of Jesse Helms to Adashevsky, who couldn't understand a word. Many people fear a military coup; I heard of one man who feared a pogrom. Art exists outside the system of critical feedback by which we know it and thus, when it is not brilliant, seems hopelessly unimproved. I asked Viktor about marriage; he said, "Simple: people need an apartment." The art crowd is the same anywhere in the world. The underlying message is not "They want what we've got." Spivak spoke of entertaining Mr. Bill Walsh and Mr. Herbert Caen; "Yes, Leningrad is good city if you like poets and mystics," he could have said to them. A man on the bus pointed out the brown, modernist KGB building with a broad grin. I hope the information I am giving you is not making you think what you are supposed to think. Russian manufacturing plants are now being converted to value in currency that can be exchanged. The Cultural Fund wants to cultivate expatriate collectors in order to initiate a more broad-scale capital return. One theory of Stalin is that he was not an artifact due to isolation from the West. After telling him I had been looking for a non-Mafia cab late Saturday night, Arkadii said over the phone, "You are in great danger; return immediately to your room." Russian X-ray scanners are not overly protected with lead. There were heaps of asbestos insulation on the street. Six-packs of Heineken bound for Taiwan were available in the hard currency bar. Looking for my missing luggage in the doorway of the carousel, I almost lost my head.

Alyosha told me that people say that Venice is the other great city. "Someday it will sink into its own mud, while Leningrad evaporates in its own light." An array of images without corresponding objects, without correlatives, wasn't alienating, although I was sad, as if grieving. The images were saturated. And my own ego was disintegrating. Just as Leningrad was named after the man who had constructed his state, so it had been named after the man who had built the city. The title of one of Ostap's paintings—not the one of two men at a table with a man-sized upright domino, but another from the same series—is *This Time We Are Both.* Sveta gave me a small pin on which she had intertwined the words St. Petersburg and San Francisco in cyrillic. And I can't say I felt split but rather, so to speak, doubled—and this was erotic. Natasha and I went into a corner of the studio during the party and showed each other pictures of our children. She was born three years after the blockade, during which her father had been a truck driver on the "Path of Freedom," the road that stretched across Lake Ladoga in the winter that froze the Germans to their hills toward Pushkin and Pavlovsk. Spivak's mother was the prima ballerina with the Kirov during those same years and, as he said, "She danced her youth every night of the blockade. Now her youth is gone, of course, and it is very unjust that Mama is excluded from the good hospitals," one of which, a yellow building set behind a fence in the heavy shadows of some trees, with deep windows and no signs of light, he pointed out. These are hospitals belonging to a *perestroika* cooperative, and one has to use hard currency to go there.

At dawn, the wire stand in front of the Bronze Horseman has not yet filled with the bouquets of today's brides. Weed-ridden palace lawn. What will this city be named later? What I am not is an expert, even of my own emotions. The telephone is not possible. Paul McCartney on the screen in the corner of the hard-currency bar. The dress code for prostitutes is international. The metal sculpture of the sailing ship is dwarfed by the terraced parking plaza in front of the glass hotel. The modesty of beggars here is startling (older women, heads shrouded, shuffling about outside of the reopened churches). I kept wondering what had become of the race of giants whose hand was visible everywhere but whose presence could be nowhere found. Even Dmitrii's large flat was a suite of small rooms. Yesterday's rain forms tiny glimmering pools across the torn-up street. To get into the exhibition, our tour guide broke through the door. You don't need to know Cyrillic to recognize Pepsi. Misha had no sooner finished explaining why he wanted a son when he learned of the birth of his daughter. Old women hold jobs just by sitting by the door. The brain is *remont.* The small, darkened lobby of the international airport was filled with Westerners cocooned into sleeping bags. Under the train station in Helsinki a cavern of shops, more product than we would see for the

Opposite page: Street scene in Leningrad.

next ten days. In Frankfurt, there's a porn arcade in the airport. The silent woman offers her glass up to each of us. Zhdanov's song drives air from the room.

> *The executioner acts as a cog between the prince and the people; the death he deals is like that of the serfs who built St. Petersburg over swamp and pestilence: It is a principle of universality; of the individual will of the despot, it makes a law for all, and of each of those destroyed bodies, a stone for the stage. It hardly matters that innocents, too, are struck down!*
>
> —Michel Foucault, *Discipline and Punish*

Over this the people's state is constructed, and over this we enter in numbers never before imagined, cameras in hand. The shops are doing a brisk business in *perestroika* fashions this Christmas. Gorby shakes the Pope's hand, and a thousand flashbulbs pop. I try to understand what Parshchikov means by the imagination as a kind of supplement that hovers in the air, once the material conditions have been accounted for. One of the papers dealt with altered states, its author professing interest in the whereabouts of Mr. Timothy Leary. I have trouble imagining the material conditions being accounted for, such that there remains the need for something beyond them. He smiles, takes a drag of his cigarette and starts again, patiently waiting for the sense we are making never to have appeared before.

On the Moscow conceptualist Backstein's t-shirt was a small sign: "You are now leaving the American sector." One might say I carry with me an instinctive antinationalism, which this message confirmed. I made a point of taking a press release for our conference to the American consulate, so that the relevant information-gathering agencies would be informed that we had arrived. In order to enter one had to get past a stiff Russian cop; inside there was a sense of chaos rather than of any efficient office design. The walls seemed to be in a permanent process of being torn apart; plaster was everywhere next to exposed studs. Our empire had been reduced to a grim outpost in a hostile state, one that I already identified more with outside. This hardly seemed in line with Emmanuel Hocquard's fit of pique at the Russian and America *rapprochement.* What in fact were we, as Americans, supposed to represent? At breakfast the French sat in a cluster and shouted "Bon appetit!" as if it were a virtual command. There was a question of which international language would be used, and plenty of complaint. At Spivak's I held out for nationalism as regression for anyone writing at the level of language. Perhaps I had no national qualities! Apparently the Russians thought the same thing about themselves. Malyavin's gloom at their collective destiny seemed universal, as if the whole world could only be seen in like terms. Isn't there a complicity with power, however at odds one may be with it, behind the sense that one is at the center of things? So what were the stakes of my nonidentity as American? For us there is no national culture to represent but a purely practical agency in the act of writing. For the Russians, a national culture must be embodied in each writer; agency rests entirely outside. Perhaps there could be an identity: the writer embodying a background condition that at the same time he or she causes to exist. But isn't that simply culture in the worst sense? Later we heard we were such interesting Americans, that our type had hitherto never been encountered by them. In any case, we survived the challenge of nonidentity just fine—but I pity the French!

There is only one word for writing in English, Ivanov said in his talk, and James Joyce found it in Russian: *krichkrov*—so I have it in the notes I was taking, illegible in parts, since I was leaning against Ron and to my left in order to hear Katya's paraphrases from behind him. He might have said *kritkrop,* the Russian for *clip-clop* (as the Russian for *woof woof* is *gav gav*), but *krich* might come from the verb *krichat',* "to cry, shout, yell, scream; to make a song (about), cry out (against)," and *krov* is the word for "roof," or "shelter." If writing is *krichkrov,* is the writer screaming on the roof, or is a poem a shelter? As recently as 1985 it was illegal in Leningrad to take photographs from a rooftop (perhaps it still is)—the slender, slightly fluted smokestack of a factory to the left of the golden cupolas over the blue towers of the St. Nicholas Cathedral and the black water of the Griboyedova Canal curving around it. Ivanov said he remembered discussing the problem of filming a dream with Tarkovsky, who insisted that dreams are a mere changing of consciousness, not its loss, and so must be seen on the screen with the clarity and precision we expect from the waking state. So the opposite of sleep is not consciousness. Tarkovsky, said Ivanov, saw of course that our life is no less capricious than dreams. Surrealism is a sovietism too. Spivak said, "This poetry is able to give a new impetus to the old idea of 'scientific poetry'—now under the guise of the practical application of the linguistics of altered states of consciousness."

To call this yogurt plain misses the point. Twenty years before, a well-known American poet wrote of his trip to South America, and of the political activities of the writers there, some of whom soon disappeared. One side of Adashevsky's business card is in English, listing his occupation as "Expert." In the photograph, Viktor and I are sitting at the small round table atop the stage—Enver's simple posters on two different colors of construction paper have been stapled to the wall behind us forming an abstract but shapely design. Later, returning in the dark from tea at Dmitrii's, we pass another gang of youths discussing passionately what violence they'd like to do the Jews. The balcony's so narrow that noboby uses it. Her job is watering the plants in the lobby of the theater, which requires her to go there for an hour twice each week. Outside the gallery is a piece by the Guerrilla Girls (I wonder if my friend A— S——— had a hand in this piece). It's no longer possible to tell the detail from the memory of the detail. The canals are impossible to tell apart. Hysteria seems an appropriate response. In our felt

Opposite page: Party at the flat of Olga Khrustalyeva, theater critic. Background: Vladimir Aristov, Moscow poet; Nikolai Kononov, Leningrad poet; Ilya Kutik. Foreground: Tadeusc Rachwal, Polish poet and member of Solidarity; Khrustalyeva.

sandals we glided over the parquet floor. Two months before, he'd been in Beijing studying the persistence of Christianity in rural communes. Outside the Hermitage a woman has set up a card table in the plaza from which she is selling tampons. Alyona, shy, provokes you to approach me on her behalf. In the back room of the basement, smaller than a water closet, was the café counter with a glass case, on the shelves of which lay small plates of sliced cucumber called salads. He leans across the table to ask me what I think of Seamus Heaney. We walk around to the side of the hotel in order to avoid the Mafia taxis. Akhmatova's penmanship is obsessive. Try to imagine: the old woman, barely able to stand, was a dancer. Without either asking or first introducing himself, the stranger (Malyavin) buys me a lunch of boiled beef and rice. I had thought to bring a repair kit for my eyeglasses. The letter *e*, on one side in English and the other Cyrillic, hung from the ribbon they had placed about Lyn's neck. Ostap liked the color scheme of the Batman T-shirt, although he had never heard of this hero. In the La Jolla supermarket, realizing that he did not even have words to go with half of the objects that he was now seeing for the first time, Arkadii grew dizzy, nauseous, faint. On one side of the room, to the right of the audience, is an unused marble fireplace. Once you board the bus, put the rice-paper ticket into the punch by the rear door to cancel it.

[Postmodernism is] about how the world dreams itself to be "American."

—Stuart Hall

I have begun to dream of being lost in Leningrad. Last night we were all about to leave, Lyn by boat, Barrett by plane, Ron by bus, and me by train. Each of us was departing for our respective stations, but I had to lug two heavy suitcases down strange streets composed of California small towns and across canals. Once I arrived at the station, with its open-air counter and platform, I stood in line until arriving at the counter whereupon the functionary wearing a KGB hat smiled and pointed at a sign. The sign suggested that I was, as usual, two hours early and thus "on time." I thanked him, picked up my heavy luggage and trudged back those same blocks and across the canals to the hotel to wait it out. Things were getting better. The night before I could not read the sign.

Suddenly, outside, underneath the window I imagined I saw his life, which now already belonged entirely to the past. I saw it move away obliquely from the window like a quiet tree-bordered street resembling the Povarskaya. And the first to take its stand in this street, by the very wall, was our State, our unprecedented and unbelievable State, rushing headlong towards the ages and accepted by them forever. It stood there below, one could hail it and take it by the hand. Its palpable strangeness somehow recalled the dead man. The resemblance was so striking that they might have been twins.

—Pasternak, *Safe Conduct*

For Pasternak, Mayakovsky's construction yielded a politics built on loss and accepted by the ages as a new meaning condensed from the possibilities of an individual life. This interpretation would seem to have gained the upper hand over Mayakovsky's intention, as the Russians I met didn't really want to talk about new meaning as a construction, certainly not in the case of Mayakovsky. Looking out the window during a storm at night after the last reading at the Composers Union, I had an irresistible urge to get to the party then in progress in the bleak apartment blocks around the Pribaltiskaya, the other modern hotel "at the windswept edge of the Baltic Sea." Trying to find a cab among disco-goers and prostitutes, I gave up after an innocuous-looking middle-aged couple wanted to drive me themselves in exchange for hard currency; the social space in between had proven too wild to traverse on a Saturday night. Later we did visit the Pribaltiskaya, a symmetrical monster surrounded by gray slabs and fronted by an enormous and deserted concrete plaza out of Fellini. Coarse grass grew between the cracks and a rusted-out manhole cover showed the date 1972 from the "period of stagnation." But I do not believe, contrary to what this juxtaposition suggests, that it makes any sense to talk about the failure of the Soviet state. In the West we would like to imagine a history that is anything but ironic, as if its conventional markers could refer back to anything but the loss of ourselves. Perhaps a state of mind could be figured on an index of possibility in another sense. It's not simply a question of our discomfort at the prospect of the socialist state being dismantled and sold to bankers from the West. I don't fully understand the difference between the ruble and hard currency, for example, except that the ruble is supposed to come with a guarantee of nonnegotiable social goods we don't get. It doesn't seem to work that way in practice, and perhaps one could speak figuratively of a tragic economics as much as the apparent economic tragedy one observes. Loss is no alternative to growth, but neither is the assessment of the real a differential calculus on which to base a maximum semantic yield. One would have to say that openness to the risk of loss of meaning can only be underwritten by belief. The Soviet state *was* a failure at the mediation of meaning, but a failure that collapsed irony and tragedy into the real. At the Russian State Museum, my favorite painting was a mural of an enormous wave, painted as a danger to be surmounted for viewers who had for the most part no experience of the sea.

Lydia Ginzburg asked me about Brodsky. Alyona had laid out the supper things for Lydia Yakovlevna—cold-smoked *gorbusha* (a small silver fish), dark bread, hard-boiled eggs, cabbage salad (salted slightly and flavored with its own juices, which are released after the cabbage is finely sliced and then squeezed and kneaded), pickled meat, horseradish, and vodka. We had toasted the formalists, and especially Tynianov, with whom Lydia Yakovlevna had worked closely from the early days of *Opoyaz.* I said that Brodsky in the West was a bourgeois lyricist, and she nodded—then laughed. "And why not?" she said, with a certain satisfaction. "If there can be socialist realism, then why not bourgeois lyrics? They are both bourgeois and gorgeous." Maybe it's capital lyricism. Her book *On Psychological Prose* in English was sitting on a chair in manuscript. "The American publisher says it is a monument," she said. I had been shown monuments in Leningrad which were now the last of their kind. I had also visited a graveyard of monuments, past a glade in a park where men were playing chess and illegally gambling, near Boris Ostanin's flat, in an area resembling a parks department maintenance yard surrounded by a high gray fence. By climbing a heap of broken concrete rubble we could look over the fence at the necropolis, where among birch trees rested some dryads, assorted damaged nymphets, male and female hero workers whose tools had been lost, three corroded Gargarins, a pile of life-sized and larger than life-sized heads of Stalin, and seventeen extended right arms and pointing forefingers of Lenin lying in a row. I felt both impious and paranoid—the high fence and warning signs meant that this wasn't an unsecret necropolis. I had a sense of "their" failure, but also of Arkadii's pleasure. No one else was around. Later Arkadii read aloud from an article in *Izvestia*. Before it was too late, a final, ultimate monument to the Soviet army had been proposed. It would represent all aspects of the army, even including a Jewish barber in a panoply of figures, gathered around a bronze tree with places in its branches for fifty birds. "Of course at its base will rest a fragment of the Kremlin Wall. There will be a lot of people. Some will attack, some will kiss a red banner, others a hammer; no one will be idle." At the center of the monument a great globe was to rest, supporting the figure of the Motherland, being bitten by the great snake of fascism, which small men would be chopping up with swords. In one hand "the Motherland has seized a shield decorated with the hammer and sickle. Her sword leans against the globe—she can't pick it up because she's already got her other hand full holding the pigeon of peace." I asked if the proposal was serious. Arkadii himself was laughing. "Why not, it is normal." There is something indeterminate about a Russian's place in history, caused by the separation between his or her simple being and his or her life. We often assume that we construct ourselves and our lives simultaneously, in the same gestures, within a continuum of options. Soviet friends enjoy pointing out the surreal effect of such constructing in their world.

4

Among the Slav communities also, money and the exchange which determines it play little or no role within the individual communities, but only on their boundaries, in traffic with others; it is simply wrong to place exchange at the centre of communal society as the original, constituent element.

—Marx

When it entered our part of the world, conceptualism discovered the total absence of any idea of the object and its inherent qualities or of any hint whatsoever of fetishization.

—Dmitrii Prigov,
"Conceptualism and the West"

Certainly I have never experienced the irrelevance of money to life more immediately than in entering the space of the Russian economy. From the beginning, when we were given an envelope containing a hundred undersized, smudged rubles, money seemed an afterthought; who pays, or anything more consequent than whether there was the right change for the bus or for mineral water, went completely by the way. Part of this sensation concerned the fact that there was literally nothing to buy; what would be bought would be either food or cheap. The tedium of waiting in line to look over art books at a museum far overshadowed any desire or need to own the object. At the end of the trip, when there was question of what to do with the leftover rubles, the natural decision was to give them to Arkadii rather than make any effort to change them—again the effort involved, the literal time, had more value than value. And then we were in a realm where time, not a metered equivalent of same, was the index of experience—and time without money expands and contracts beyond one's preconception. The wait in line and the abrupt change of plans were the new units of value

Opposite page: View of the Hotel Pribaltiskaya through the window of a bus.

against which our time would be measured and displaced. What this reorientation does to the thought of community—what we have always wanted to imagine at the opposite end of the exchanges that tie us down to some material fate—was very present in our immediate reorientation. A particular anxiety surrounding value had been removed, raising the value of possibilities for what occurs. (Later, after I told her this impression, Carla said, "It must be like a kind of theatrical time." It is undivided.)

Even as I speak, the language translates my intention. "That's not interesting," said Viktor, refusing to convey even the gist of Yulia's talk on the mythology of Stalinism, meaning not her presentation but the problem of Stalin. "He's out of left field," said Arkadii of the questioner at my talk, he and Viktor both refusing to translate, the fellow later approaching me in the dark cellar corridor of Shostakovich's old union hall to pose it in his own thick English: "You speak as one who comes from a land of objects, therefore it is easy for you to conceive of language as an object, as objective, whereas we do not." After the formal luncheon with its unintelligible toasts, we were bundled onto a tour bus and driven to the apartment complex where Shklovsky had lived. Zhdanov closed his eyes and appeared to sing. On the street, to avoid robbery, we learned to respond to the question "Are you Americans?" with *"Je suis français."* Kutik translated as fast as he could, three of us crowded hopelessly under one umbrella in the pouring rain, but the real communication was much more direct—your eyes were a perfect blue.

I have what might be called an intuition or simple vague sense of the aptness, of a relationship between money and time, but a relationship between money and space (in the abstract, so the spatial) seems less necessary. Unless, of course, one thinks of space as property, as real estate. But Soviet space can't be possessed. And despite their love of the peculiar and almost material light in which their city floats, always only partially visible, very many of the Russians in Leningrad (and many Russians everywhere), so I've been told more than once, are agoraphobes. They are afraid, in this and other contexts, of infinity. And I remember my first experiences of the social space in Soviet buses and the interrelationships of people in crowds. In a crowded American bus, each person tries to contract, so as to occupy a minimum amount of space, out of courtesy, and to avoid contact, out of fear. In a crowded French or Italian bus (I can speak only from real experience) people exert a more lascivious, less decorous, pressure against each other, but more from efficiency than sensuality. But on a crowded Soviet bus, I have felt myself, so to speak, embraced, almost maternally, standing among people who seem to expand to support each other in the lurching bus and together assume the burden of heavy cloth and plastic bags pressed between them. The experience was comforting. In August I noted to Arkadii and Zina that Americans try to diminish in crowds and Russians try to expand. "Oy, I hate our people in buses. Everyone makes themselves as big as possible and the air smells horrible," said Zina. "I always have fights because I try to open some windows. And they hate open windows."

We know of the desire for the object but what of the object's desire for us? Returning to Frankfurt we stand in line waiting to show our passports. The periphery of the vast waiting area is lined with shops selling everything from expensive leather handbags and designer clothing to Japanese electronic gadgets, liquor, and fountain pens. The commercial signage mixes with functional blue-and-white airport directions, creating a huge textual mobile that shimmers in every direction. It is the most common Western panorama, and yet after the relative absence of all such information in Russia, its sudden reappearance creates a kind of vertigo. Something "needs" us in the sense that nature, in the nineteenth century, needed poets to articulate the speechless. One stands in awe before a battery-operated pants press, a computer that remembers what day it is in Jakarta, a telephone shaped like a billiard ball.

Prigov's confidence that Russian conceptualism takes place in a culture without any notion of the object leads one to wonder what could be its organizing dynamic. Several visual artists I met seemed rather extreme in their sense of knowing the value of objects, likewise—for one, Natasha Swalow, who introduced herself as the president of the "Women Admirers of Jeff Koons Club." She had met Ronald Feldman. The club meets frequently to discuss topics in the postmodern. I tried to give her a sense of why Jeff Koons was thought by many in the West to be problematic in his relation to the market; Natasha expressed no reluctance or guilt whatsoever in embracing it. "So you want Russia to be carved up into bite-sized real-estate chunks and sold to the West?" Did she know that when Clement Greenberg distinguished between avant-garde and kitsch, his main referent for kitsch was the Stalinist cult of mediocrity? We observed that the "People's Artist" who had given the lengthy and interrupted banquet toast might well be cast in silver as a kitsch work by Koons, not to mention his Pushkin statue. There is, in fact, an endless reservoir of mediocre objects circulating in Russian social space.

Opposite page: Nadezhda Kondakova, Moscow poet.

Against a background of cheap prints, lace doilies, plastic wind-up toys, Pushkin fountain pens, Rosa Televisor, a nineteen-year-old sculptor whose broken, rusted chains showed possibility in the "Women and Art" exhibition, sat still with eyes straight ahead and perfectly composed expression when Natasha expediently removed the Langton catalogue I had given Rosa from her hands (just for safekeeping?). Later Natasha's conceptual artist husband, Enver, went on at length in Russian without translation in hope that I would perhaps carry his views on the postmodern with me back to the West. He seemed to convey an immanent explanation for everything.

In the room beyond the Gauguins stood the casket of Alexander Nevsky. In the curiously lush, pink-walled restaurant of the Architects Union, waiting two hours for our tough boiled beef to arrive, preceded only by a small plate of cut-up tomato covered in something that might be an equivalent to Thousand Island dressing, Zhdanov gulps his champagne, bums a steady stream of Opals from Kutik, and reads aloud from an English phrase book, the questions ("Do you dye your hair?" "Is that your mother?" "Can you fix my muffler?") directed to no one at all, intended only to occupy space. Michael and I walked on ahead. The Winter Palace's long outer walls were an intense lime-sherbet green, broken only by the white trim, the ornamental windows, and the palest light I have ever seen. "Lozhka," you said slowly, picking it up from the saucer, your lips careful to form each phoneme as I replied just as slowly, "Spoon." An apple the size of a lemon, the color of a potato. "What's being repaired at the Lenin Museum?" "Lenin."

But what is feminism? In the West feminism originates with the unease pertaining to women's object status (an object which, as if by definition, warrants devaluation), and this in turn has something to do with the description of women (and the identity of her describers). In Russia I was asked frequently about feminism, what it was; isn't Meryl Streep in *Kramer vs. Kramer* a comic character, since she has her own flat, not a communal one, and a husband who isn't a drunk, and wonderful appliances? Her discontent is incredible, illogical—it's funny; what more could there be? There were seven young village women seated very close together in the bath gossiping and we joined them silently, because of being so cold. One evening I had invited three women friends to the hard-currency restaurant at a hotel, and while we talked one was eating spoonfuls of plain butter from the butter dish. Feminism is for Western women who have leisure for such things. On another occasion Lyuda Davidova asked me the same question: What is feminism? On the night before Lent, which comes at the beginning of spring and is regarded as a period for purification, so that everyone observes their own particular rules of fasting, it is traditional to sit late with friends and feast on blini. Lyuda was standing at the stove tending the skillet, the focus of conversation, repeatedly refilling a platter with thin pancakes which we were eating with jam or marinated fish while drinking wine or vodka. In the bath one woman cupped her breasts in her hands, then ran them down her sides over her naked stomach, while the other women laughed, and rested them on her thighs. Maybe for Soviet women feminism will develop out of the unease resulting from the established myth that the workplace is a Soviet woman's second real home. She is then a Stalinist icon, with a strong sense of homelessness in the state's symbolic order. From the end of the table Valerii offered me a candy from his pocket—he shared a studio with Ostap, and just the day before I had seen his ironic realist paintings of goldfish and empty bottles. "You would be beautiful," said one of the village women, "maybe, but you're too thin." A third woman rested her hand on my arm and then counted the folds of flesh between her breasts and her pubic hair. The object of value in this social setting was the bottle of shampoo from the West. I was thinking about this scene late one night when the men were being irritable, since we hadn't eaten very much all day, and we now found ourselves going along to someone's flat for tea instead of to the hotel whose restaurant would close in an hour. Our host when inviting us for tea had merely said that perhaps his wife might prepare a "traditional Russian pie of apples" which she and he had picked the week before in Pushkin's garden.

"Women in Russia are things," Katya responded to my question about feminism. "Oh well, there is an official women's movement, but all it says is that women are good, that motherhood is good, that everything is fine the way it is."

"But is there an 'unofficial' feminist movement?" I asked.

"Yes, but I'm not sure where it is."

"You mean you don't know the address—surely there is some sort of underground connection?"

"No, I mean that no one knows where it is," she replied.

"But maybe the lack of information means that things really *are* good—that the issues of concern to women in the West have been solved. I've heard that the majority of doctors, for example, are women."

"That's true," she said, "but I would never go to one of them if I were pregnant."

"Why not?"

"Because they are no good. Nobody respects them, they are underpaid and the facilities are terrible."

"Well, should I send you some feminist literature when I get back home, then?"

"What I'd really like, if you wouldn't mind sending it, would be the collected poems of Jim Morrison."

What is an object and where do I find one in Russia? On a Monday afternoon in August the Nevsky Prospekt is jammed with shoppers carrying plastic bags with little in them. At late afternoon, the neighborhood where Dostoyevsky lived stands for a melancholy to which the visitor is referred. A modernist-looking political poster in red advertises a meeting of the Popular Front. Gostinii Dvor is *remont,* opening the next decade. Like Nixon in the early seventies, Gorbachev has extracted surplus value by lowering the standard of living, but in his case not to finance a war. As I walked past a couple embracing on a side street at midnight, the man reached out and grabbed hold of my coat. Detskii Mir, the central and only toy store, contained cardboard boxes full of cheap plastic sand toys (and wooden blocks). The former Fabergé store on Gertsena remains a jewelry store, possibly for newlyweds with the requisite slips of paper, all the merchandise at one end with the rest of the space for people to wait. Viktor Malyavin sighed deeply to confirm a Nietzschean view of some kind of end of the world. At night the bridges on the Neva are raised, making ambulance traffic from one side of the city to

Opposite page: Leningrad alley.

the other impossible. An entirely rusted manhole cover in the enormous, cracked cement plaza outside the Pribaltiskaya showed a date: 1972. The proto-fascist party Pamyat's (Memory) poster was defaced with a swastika. The "Period of Stagnation" having ended, what is most notably lacking exactly defines the social horizon. Several hundred of the avant-garde viewed film parodies of Soviet survivalism (bare-assed youths crawling through barbed wire in the snow) with gales of laughter, a sense of release. There is no "covering myth" as we would identify it, but the continued production of wildly divergent forms of belief irregardless is something Blake would understand. This is why vegetarians and Esperantists were so threatening to Stalin.

By now I was no longer certain which part of the city we were in, still following the winding Neva. "That is the dacha where Nixon stayed," said the little man. He slumbers on the couch in the minuscule living room, while in the bedroom sleep his wife and grown son. Were these youth, the Katzenjammer Kids, supposed to be fascist punks or the parody of fascist punks—the vague hues of the television screen merely suggested the presence of color, Finnish subtitles lost in a bleached-out landscape. As midnight nears, Barrett and Lyn rush to the airport to greet their luggage. Parshchikov decides that he is the one to hold the conversation together (and, in retrospect, he was entirely correct). The hospital grounds were lonely, almost empty even during the humid afternoons, so that the spectre of these Afghan-shattered soldiers' bodies was tangible more by its displacement of space—much more than an American city block—than by any lingering visible insistence. Quickly one learns to search out the skyline for the gold spire. Outside St. Isaacs, I found a hard-currency hamburger stand on wheels, the term for which is *fastfoodski.* But how is a marriage of convenience possible in a one-room apartment? Alyona's excessive flattery was the opposite of seductive. Next to the Stalinist bureaucrat-sculptor who was learning, reluctantly, to accommodate an avant-garde (Rosa Televisor's name was not Rosa Televisor), these two American graduate students prospecting a new terrain simply because it had yet to be staked out were rank amateurs. These racist epithets are directed specifically at Parshchikov, who refuses to look up, methodically chewing his meal. They hover outside the Beriozhka, waiting for the Americans to exit with their American coins. Here stand two brick columns, each adorned with the figure of Neptune at its base. The rain had made the unpaved street here in the center of town almost impassable, so people simply grabbed boards from the neighboring construction project and built a gangway to the ornate doorway of the Composers Union. This is an unofficial issue of the official journal, *Theater Life.*

The pretext for initiating the overthrow of the Stalinist old guard in Leningrad began with a move to expose and then stop the mismanagement and embezzlement of money designated for the control of the Neva. Romanov was ousted from the top position in the city and shortly thereafter from the Politburo. His grand scheme to dam and straighten the river was bankrupt before work began, but not before establishing at least the pretense that it was planned. At one place along the embankment, an older bulky stone pillar is set along the concrete balustrade, and on top of the pillar rests a massive concrete ball, or monster sphere, plain, except for the pits eroded on its surface. It's impossible to decide what it represents; it's monumental, not decorative. Perhaps it symbolizes the moon, the earth, or some abstraction like "the world." Because of its position at an overlook along the embankment, it's ominous—it threatens to roll off the pillar and crush someone gazing at the Neva. But the engineering feat that keeps it balanced on its pillar is nothing compared to the feat which maintains the Triumphal Column in Revolution Square, elevated not with mortar but by gravity alone. I imagine us triangulating our descriptions on the elements (context-object-content) involved. Now there are shortages but there's no miserliness in these Soviet scenes. (To survey them, said Dziubenko, a new group of physicist literary theorists have established *Versus Universus,* a magazine.)

Then there is the "object" of our visit: to participate in a conference dealing with . . . what? "Language—Consciousness—Society: The Problems of Contemporary Culture," as the letter of invitation states. We hear papers on everything from altered states of consciousness to the modernity of Joyce to the semiotics of Stalinist art to poetics. Our common "capital" is our willingness to participate, but there are problems with the mode of exchange. The question-and-answer sessions after each presentation seem lively, but when Barrett asks an important question after a talk, there is little follow-up. The most interesting discussion happens in the corridors or in the café downstairs. In such moments another commodity is exchanged, more ephemeral because part of some economy whose currency is elusive. Viktor Lapitsky wants to link what I have said in my talk to Derrida—well, yes and no. Enver thinks Jameson is really against Marxism because he makes so many qualifications of it. Well, yes and no. While we're standing in line for coffee, somebody introduces himself as the editor of a new theory magazine, and the first issue could deal with Karl Popper. Would I like to contribute? Well, yes and no. Although the smoke is suffocating in these rooms, one works to "get it right," to clarify or redefine or redirect the question, not to mystify, to be generous but not uncritical, to be fair, to be outrageous. It seems like our last chance. One fails.

Arkadii and I are standing on the bus as we ride to his apartment in the suburbs. In the middle of our conversation he interrupts and points out the half-destroyed brick buildings in this part of Leningrad. He explains that they were built as an experiment in which apartments and factories would be combined in communal work-living arrangements. In recent years they have fallen into disrepair, and many of the factories have closed down. Now there are portions between the buildings where grass and trees are growing wild. "I love this," Arkadii says, referring to the riot of vines and plants that have dug into the deserted works, "I like these empty places."

Later, walking to his apartment through the wide expanse of grass in front of the considerably newer buildings, I ask Arkadii to stop so that I can take his picture. There is no one in sight in all directions; even his apartment is hidden behind trees. There is just Arkadii standing with a smile that seems almost sheepish but which signals his pleasure at the general activity of things this week. There is no one in sight, we are saying nothing, the rain that has been falling intermittently all day has now stopped, and although it is gray, the air is fresh. I take his picture.

When Dreiser went to the Soviet Union in the thirties, he saw the future "and it is now." Wittgenstein surreptitiously visited at about the same time and reported nothing, although his students found him obsessed with an ethics that could be reduced to mechanical functioning (a seeming analogy to the communist state). Would it matter in the same sense what contemporary poets would think of the Soviet Union, now that its heroic period has ended? What we would see could never be reduced to a single image or expression. Underneath the image register that is our privileged index of knowing lie long-dormant functionalist explanations, utopian machines that our learned Marxism, for example, would try to recover as a language. These explanations have been countered and negated, thoroughly woven into a cultural matrix that is an image of directed stasis through which real, temporal powers push and pull. In what way is the modernist sensitivity that supposedly feels and responds through this deadlock anything more than an adjunct component of a well-functioning machine? A machine that has

Opposite page: Sculptor M. K. Anikushin, creator of Leningrad's Pushkin statue and several Lenin figures, giving a toast. To his left: Katya Dobrovskaya and Michael Davidson. Across, left to right: Valerii Zayayev; Arkadii Dragomoshchenko; Barrett Watten; Ron Silliman; Henri Deluy; Natalia Strizhevskaya, Moscow poet and translator; and Emmanuel Hocquard.

played out its creativity until it produces nothing more than itself in a temporal sequence of images. If we were to write in a sequence of virtual images perhaps we would recover, by formal means, the explanations that had produced them. This would seem to be the explanatory moment of the New Sentence, for example. But what of our explanations once we have encountered an entirely different set of beliefs? Perhaps the explanation of the Soviet Union that we have obtained is immanent to our understanding (it was, in some sense, there all along)—"the language" had been responding to it in the time even before we were (Dreiser's utopia and Wittgenstein's silence). Belief makes language, not the other way around. That is why, in the Soviet Union, language at the present time is billowing out of proportion, being driven by beliefs that have outstripped their terms. "The people" stands for one such belief, originally manufactured on religious grounds and desperately looking for new expression. The utopian scientism of the poetics conference would be one of its adjuncts—where technique and pure subjectivity merge (a possibility in Russian art at least since Malevich). Our horizon, blocked at all points in a series of managed substitutions, meets its counterpart in an infinitely expanding horizon that can envision no negation. Down on the ground it looked like a human universe, even if from moment to moment a fantastic refiguring of incommensurate beliefs.

"I will live with that broken basin until the end of my days," says the mother. Arkadii is brewing tea in his son's studio, an abandoned communal flat. The ground crew at the airport are soldiers—they stand with their hands pressed flat over their ears as our bulky Aeroflot taxies slowly in. Ostap, in his new black-and-red Batman T-shirt. In *Little Vera,* an all-too-believable instance of the dysfunctional family is seen as hemmed in by a lack of available alternatives. If you stand next to the ticket punch on the bus, people will expect you to validate their tiny rice-paper five-kopek passes. United thought nothing of canceling the flight to Los Angeles. Her fiancé locks the drunken father into the bathroom. Dinner in Helsinki at the Magic Pan. Zina Dragomoshchenko is the hero of this tale. From this two-lane rural road we could see the twin cones of the cooling towers just to the east of the city. I give you the one book of my poetry I have left. Before, I could not have said what I expected to find. The architect lunged to grab at the waitress's ass only to fall sprawling from his chair, friends trudging slowly over to lift him back into it, from which he then ordered (and received) yet another bottle. So he simply stabs the would-be son-in-law. The Germans' desire for the city as an object in a game of unilateral exchange is not erasable—Olga's aunt raises her glass—while the Germans themselves appear abstract (they never arrived). What I could not discern was a hierarchy of color: Is a blue palace better than a red one? Without warning (without meaning) a fight breaks out in the park. A typical story concerned the woman who called the police to complain of brutality by her husband and when they arrived moaned over and over that she had a nail in her head, who was then taken off and placed into long-term psychiatric care until one day a therapist, in a supportive gesture, ran his hands through her hair and discovered, to his surprise, the small nail her husband had literally beaten into her skull. Enver's poem is thrust into my hand in a blue envelope, as if taking it west was a form of publication. Admit that Lenin was wrong on the national question. The old widows begging outside of the churches demonstrate history. The occasion of tea is a surreal potlatch. Passives lurk behind manic verbs. Zhdanov stands beside the piano in the ornate drawing room and begins to sing in his pure Siberian baritone generic statements from an English phrasebook. These beautiful women with their terrible teeth. Ilya leads me to the table of his friends, the context of a local poetry scene immediately familiar—the event at the bar after a reading in any small college town—and one of them, a tall, bearlike young man, leans forward to glare into my eyes, asking, "What do you think of Seamus Heaney?" Sentences in a paragraph like residents in a communal flat: either there's a hierarchy or you negotiate. I pass Ostap's medal on—"veteran of labor"—with its single condition (that it can only be possessed for one month and must be handed on to a "hero") still intact. Passions lurk behind manic poets. Outside of the hotels, we're hustled back into the black Volgas and given an immediate, hurried tour of the city. At this latitude one begins to comprehend the slow, deliberate motion of bears. I remember a year earlier panic in the voice of Irene Kiss, a Hungarian critic, panhandled by two blacks at the Ashby BART: How could this occur in a free country? Not able to cry, an emotion is suspended in time, butting up against everything. Cherubs and lions look down at us from the green walls of the Winter Palace. The airport lobby is a single room, like some drab rural Greyhound station, full of sleepers in sleeping bags—larvae in the night. As little as possible, I want to reply. These thugs cannot imagine that the role they have chosen to play is not their own invention. Red tile walls on the platform of Mayakovsky Station: doors like those on an elevator open to let you on the train (the drivers of which cannot see the station, living entirely in their endless tunnel). Who will remember the lamb kabob over rice? Setting, the sun catches the gold of the spire just right. Each of us fantasizes how to get Michael out of the line of fire, just in case. In the final scene, the father slumps to the floor, drunken or dying. Rigorous though it is, Ilya's translation is a convenient fiction—we're not discussing the role of word-of-mouth at all. The bridges are raised after dark. Dystopias of the world unite!

Without objects to organize, one doesn't develop a strong sense of organization, nor a method which stretches events taut over the framework of time. So the afternoon's talks (Grigorii Tulochinsky on "Culture and Mythocracy," Boris Ostanin on "The Metonymic Reading of the Symbol," and Vladislav Kushov on "Natural Language and the Language of Quantum Physics"), which were scheduled to end at four, were still going on—finally at 6:30 we went out into the rain and mud along Gertsena, past Nabokov's windows—with a sense of intense but aimless agency. They say, "If you race down the slope bare-assed, you'll have to stop yourself with your prick." Consistently our friends expressed articulate solicitude for us, informed by their sense of the West and of what we might expect, which served to reorient me repeatedly, within their proprietary terms, imagined as the invasion of solace. Halfway through that second week of August, Zina had a dream about her workplace, a movie theater at a corner bus stop along the 100 line (which ends in front of the Finland Station), where she worked as the gardener tending plants growing in containers in the lobbies of all three levels of the theater. Because of the dream, she went to work the next day around noon, to water the plants and wash dirt off the leaves, and we didn't see her until six at the conference. "I always go to work the day after I dream about it," she said. That produced an image of a

"Sonnet to Improve the World." We were crowded together again the next afternoon, some drinking mineral water saturated with iron that had turned to rust and the rest drinking cognac in the humid cobalt basement room of the Composers Union with Viktor, Katya, and Arkadii, passing around manuscripts. Where we say, "He straddles the fence," they say, "He sits with a chair for each cheek." And when we say, "The man is a crook," they say that "the man is a corner."

REVEALING DEVICES

> *I am this month one whole year older than I was this time twelve-month; and having got, as you perceive, almost into the middle of my fourth volume—and no farther than to my first day's life—'tis demonstrative that I have three hundred and sixty-four days more life to write just now, than when I first set out. . . .*
>
> —Lawrence Sterne, *Tristram Shandy*

The name of our hosting institution, "Poetic Function," pays homage to *Opoyaz* teachings, particularly the idea that poetry makes the familiar strange. As strangers, we invert the terms, imposing a map upon an unfamiliar landscape. Within one day, Barrett was able to orient himself with respect to the Baltic. An object by any other name is not a cutlet, as we discovered upon ordering. The three channels play three men talking. Ron affixed stick-on labels bearing the Russian equivalents for various objects in the room. I had been told to bring a bathroom sink stopper for which there was no equivalent. Lyn wore a letter around her neck. The lights in the restaurant were on, but there was no food. "Why does it stay open?" I asked Malyavin. "Because we are a developing country," he replied.

On our tour of the city, we stop in front of Shklovsky's apartment. On another corner is the "House of Silence" where Brodsky and other émigrés once lived. We then drive through the neighborhood described in *Crime and Punishment* and pass the house where Akhmatova lived during her later years. Pushkin's name is a shrine. Lenin's armored car is a statue in a public park. Nabokov's windows look out on a street under repair. In reading *St. Petersburg* by Bely late at night in the hotel, I recognize many of the buildings and waterways. In the car, the map is useless; things pass by too quickly to be assimilated.

On the last day, we meet with the official cultural foundation representative who has invited us for tea. We are given large posters depicting early Russian icons. One has come to expect the bottles of mineral water whose rusty taste has become rather familiar. Outside, while waiting for the bus, friends from the conference appear from nowhere and hand us letters to be mailed upon our return. There is no way for them to pay postage, but they include stamps anyway, several of which depict beautiful antique samovars. In the period since these things have happened, other things have taken their place. It is difficult knowing which tense to use. Institutions have changed their names, and certain persons no longer remain in power. The Western press likes to speak of "unbelievable changes," changes occurring "almost daily," but this is to make change inevitable, the fulfillment of a design. One samovar resembles an old-fashioned steam turbine.

Our friends have stayed up all night, preparing us a late dinner and then driving us to the airport before dawn to catch our plane. The lights in the terminal are not yet on, and other passengers sleep on benches or piles of luggage. The whole scene resembles a bus station in a small town in Nebraska rather than the central terminal of a major international airport. We exchange quiet good-byes with Arkadii and Adashevsky, and they go back to the cabs and drive off. We settle down and wait for the lights to come on.

Michael Davidson is the author of several volumes of poetry and the historical study, *The San Francisco Renaissance: Poetics and Community at Mid-Century.* He is now a professor of literature at the University of California at San Diego.

Lyn Hejinian, author of numerous books of poetry, is coeditor of the critical annual *Poetics Journal.*

Ron Silliman is a member of the *Socialist Review* editorial collective. He is the author of thirteen books of poetry and one of criticism and the editor of an anthology of language poetry.

Barrett Watten is the author of a major theoretical volume, *Total Syntax,* plus many books of poetry. He is coeditor of *Poetics Journal* and associate editor of the journal *Representations.*